SELF-EMPOWERMENT:
AWAKENING THE POWER WITHIN

By

ROSELLE THOMPSON

EAGLE PUBLICATIONS

Published by Eagle Publications
Unit 100560, P O Box 6945, London W1A 6US, England.
A Paperback Original
First published in the United Kingdom in 2025

Text copyright © 2025 Roselle Thompson

The right of Roselle Thompson to be identified as the Author of this work has been asserted by her.

ISBN 978-18381068-8-1

A CIP catalogue record for this book is available from the British Library
All rights Reserved
This book is sold subject to the condition that it shall not by way of trade or otherwise, be lent, hired out or otherwise circulated in any form of binding or cover other than that in which it is published. No part of this publication may be reproduced, stored in a retrieval system, or transmitted in any form or by any means (electronic, mechanical, photocopying, recording or otherwise) without the prior written permission of Eagle Publications.

All paper used by Eagle Publications is SFI (Sustainable Forestry Initiative) and PEFC (Programme for the Endorsement of Forest Certification Schemes) Certified.

This is a work of fiction. Names, characters, incidents and dialogues are products of the author's imagination or are used fictitiously. Any resemblance to actual people, living or dead, events or locales is entirely coincidental.

Printed in the United Kingdom and United States by Lightning Source for Eagle Publications

www.eaglepublications.org.uk

CONTENTS

ABOUT THIS BOOK 5
INTRODUCTION 9
PART I: FOUNDATIONS OF INNER AWAKENING 19
    CHAPTER 1 **UNDERSTANDING YOUR INNER POWER** 20
    CHAPTER 2 **AFFIRMATIONS – Beyond limitations** 40
    CHAPTER 3 **ROADBLOCKS – RELEASING WHAT KEEPS YOU SMALL** 53
PART II – THE INNER SHIFT: THOUGHT, EMOTION § ENERGY 185
    CHAPTER 4 **Understanding Mindset** 186
    CHAPTER 5 **The Mindset Shift – Transforming Your Thought Patterns** 194
    CHAPTER 6 **Coming Home to the Now** 201
    CHAPTER 7 **Emotional Intelligence: Honouring Your Feelings as Guides** 210
    CHAPTER 8 **The Energy Within – Aligning with Higher Vibrations** 218
PART III – EMBODIMENT OF POWER AND PURPOSE 225
    CHAPTER 9 **Embodying Confidence – Trusting Yourself Deeply** 226
    CHAPTER 10 **Boundaries and Integrity – Protecting Your Peace** 232
    CHAPTER 11 **Navigating Fear – From Paralysis to Power** 240
PART IV – EXPANSION AND CONTRIBUTION 250

CHAPTER 12 **Creating a Vision – Aligning with Your Future Self** 251

CHAPTER 13 **Empowered Relationships – Leading with Love & Truth** 255

CHAPTER 14 **The Ripple Effect – Living as a Lighthouse** 259

CHAPTER 15 **Full Circle – Becoming the Embodied Self** 263

CHAPTER 16 **30-DAY EMPOWERMENT CHALLENGE** 267

REFERENCES 273

RECOMMENDED READING & RESOURCES 275

ABOUT THIS BOOK

PART I – FOUNDATIONS OF INNER AWAKENING

Part 1 of this book, identifies and interrogates various roadblocks that are common barriers which tend to invade your efforts to self-improvement, and negatively stifle your potential to tap into the power that lies within you. At the same time, as a counter measure to roadblocks, we interrogate each roadblock and highlight the individual solutions to each one.

I also introduce a model I designed entitled, **Self-Empowerment Excellence Model (SEEM),** © to help individuals tap into their inner power, to shift from a problem-focused and reactive lifestyle to a more empowered and creative way of living in our world. This Model, which has its background in over 30 years of my teaching of academic students, (many of whom had complex issues leading to barriers to them accessing the curriculum), was developed from a previous Excellence Model I had created, for correcting behaviour issues. Embodied in this previous *Challenging Behaviour Excellence model (2009)* were culturally sensitive and socially specific approaches to dealing with the children, who were displaying a variety of challenging behaviours that made it difficult for them to engage in their learning. The success criteria of this previous Excellence Model are based on the triangular pillars of this current **Self-Empowerment Excellence Model (SEEM)**, © and provides proof that its tripartite structure, (embodying **Self-awareness, Self-discipline** and **Positive mindset),** has its correlative in developing evidence-based, self-empowerment principles, that enable an individual to tap into their inner power.

At the **end of Part 1,** you are invited to take a self-assessment tool with an explanation of scores, that is designed to help you reflect on the state of your current mindset. It will also help to identify areas for improvement, so that you can take actionable steps toward cultivating a growth-oriented perspective in your life.

PART II – THE INNER SHIFT: THOUGHT, EMOTION & ENERGY

Part 2 gets to the heart of practices of **self-discipline,** because you already have an **awareness** of how to eradicate roadblocks as they show up, in the detailed discussions given in Part 1 of the book. Therefore, Part 2, takes you through practical steps, via more informal and inspirational conversations that you will resonate with, as motivational approaches to developing your positive mindset.

Each part of this book presents the practicality of applying the **Self-Empowerment Excellence Model (SEEM)**© in developing self-empowerment, as we move from transforming limiting beliefs to cultivating a growth mindset, with deep inner meaning via practical tools. In Chapter 7, you will be shown how to expand your understanding, by honouring and using your emotions as sacred messengers, not obstacles. The exercises and principles presented are designed to encourage maturity and emotional resilience.

In addition, Chapter 8 introduces energetic alignment, frequency, and vibrational awareness. This section helps you to shift your internal state, in order to magnetise opportunities and peace, in your self-empowerment journey.

PART III – EMBODIMENT OF POWER AND PURPOSE

Part 3 of this book shows you how to harness an embodiment of power and purpose. This section is designed to empower you to stop waiting and start choosing. It also encourages you to be responsible without feeling ashamed. The idea is for you to experience freedom through self-leadership and conscious choice, because no journey to self-empowerment is complete without this experiential learning. At the same time, **Part 3** helps you to cultivate authentic self-confidence, based on alignment, not ego. Additionally, I encourage you to trust in your intuition, voice and presence, via some practical exercises that develop your inner knowledge. Some exercises teach you how to practice the importance of boundaries as spiritual self-respect. The fact is, saying *"no"* with grace is not rejection, it's actually discerning *'yes'* with clarity, and aligning with integrity.

PART IV – EXPANSION & CONTRIBUTION

The final section of this book, **Part 4**, supports an expansion and contribution to your self-empowerment practice, and includes helping you to uncover your deeper purpose. Chapter 16 offers reflection tools and principles to live with clarity, meaning and service. This final section of the book also shifts relationship dynamics from co-dependency and performance to mutual empowerment and scared connection.

Then as we move into the final chapter, you are invited to become the light – living as an empowered presence, with a call to embody the transformation. Then finally, I encourage you to walk the path of self-empowerment with humility, courage and grace, as I offer a reflection on the ripple effect of personal power.

INTRODUCTION

From the moment we are born, we begin to absorb the narratives of others. We are taught who we should be, how we should act, what is acceptable, and what is not. These stories often begin with love or protection, but over time, they become layers we mistake for truth.

Many of these beliefs live in our unconscious minds:

- *"I'm not good enough."*
- *"I always mess things up."*
- *"I don't deserve success."*

These are not facts. They are inherited patterns. And the moment we become aware of them; we are free to rewrite them.

Releasing limiting beliefs is not about denying pain or pretending life has been easy. It is about choosing a new relationship with your past. One that allows you to carry the wisdom forward while leaving the weight behind.

Start by identifying one belief that no longer serves you. Ask yourself:

- *Where did this belief come from?*

- *Is it absolutely true?*
- *Who would I be without it?*

The truth is that healing begins with honesty, and empowerment begins with choice. You are not your wounds, but you are the one who is healing, so let's begin by exploring what self-empowerment is and how you tap into the power that lies within you.

In this book, self-empowerment is firstly explored by using a set of unique, self-development principles, based on a **Self-Empowerment Excellence Model© (SEEM)**, which I designed to help individuals tap into their inner power, to shift from a problem-focused and reactive lifestyle to a more empowered and creative way of living in our world. This Model is examined in detail later, as we look at its inextricable link to mindset, discipline, awareness, and behavioural transformation.

However, to make this shift, several steps must be taken in a journey of self-discovery, to realise that there is a fusion of basic principles that we practice daily, which are constantly creating our reality, whether it's happy or sad. It works like this - what we think about (our thoughts), is where we always put our focus. For example, consider this for a moment - when you are happy, or in love, or sad, or excited, that particular focus <u>always</u> engages your emotions. Then, depending on which emotion is dominating your mind at the time, it will ultimately influence the way you behave.

Now, think back to times in your own life, when you experienced different emotions and how you behaved as a result, as you created the same experiences, day after day. These may be experiences of struggle and strife, where you are continually looking for solutions from outside of yourself. So, the scenario is, you wake up with the same thoughts that trigger the same emotions, which drive the same behaviours and create the same experience day after day.

The sad fact is, you can't change what you are not aware of, and awareness is the first step to breaking free from automated patterns that have been running your life on auto pilot. The good news is, you are about to break that cycle of limitations when you become consciously empowered, to awaken your inner power. This is not about temporary motivation; this is about permanent transformation.

Every great achievement in human history, every breakthrough, every innovation and every triumph, began with an awareness and understanding of the individual's ability to tap into their inner power, in ways that defied their current reality. Therefore, my excitement is for you to become aware of the interconnectedness and dynamic relationship between your thoughts, your emotions and your behaviour; even the way you are feeling right now. The fact is, once you've learnt about the steps to self-empowerment, and the roadblocks that have the potential to impede your path to empowerment and the power within you, an optimum level of awareness will be reached. At that level, you will gain clarity about how a fusion of this dynamic relationship can work to create your ideal desires. It's also at that point, you can say you have awakened to the power that lies within! Are you ready? Because once you understand this and truly apply the principles of my **Self-Empowerment Excellence Model© (SEEM)**, there's no going back to your old self!

So, welcome to your special journey of empowerment, to awake the power within you! The fact that you are here today, is a good sign – it is the first step to awakening that power or giant that lies within you! They say that *'knowledge is power '*– I would go one step further and say that *'knowing how to harness that power within,'* is indeed what *power* really is. It is why I'm very excited to share this knowledge with you in this book. It means that together, by dissecting what self-empowerment is, and delving into this transformative topic, will reveal your potential to change your life and awaken to *the power within you*.

This subject is not new, many examples exist in the history of our world, our country, our town, our village, our families - where individuals have tapped into their individual power within, and have become shining examples of either doing what might seem to others to be impossible; undertaking great feats in the face of immense danger; showing fortitude where defeat seemed to be the only alternative; or have inspired others to overcome situations in the face of a groundswell of adversities throughout their lives.

In other words, both history and culture have given us examples, based on the facts we know and teach others about, from our home settings to educational setting; that there is indeed an identifiable power within us which, when tapped into, make some individuals seem uniquely gifted, so they are categorised as heroes, heroines, and *"special"* in some way.

The question is, why is this power more prominent in some than in others? Well, answers to this question will be revealed as we journey along the road to your own self-discovery. At the outset, there is one basic fact we can agree with, and that is the existence of an ever-present power, in every single one of us; and that this power is always readily available to be tapped into, at will. Unfortunately, it remains dormant to some, or undiscovered by others, and this may be due to their lack of awareness that it exists. In fact, most people treat the subject in a flippant way, denying its presence, while others blatantly reject its reality and effectiveness altogether.

However, whether acknowledged or not, the fact is, there is an incredible power within you. And its dynamism can transform your circumstances beyond anything you have ever imagined. Indeed, it is also a fact that being inside you, this power is just waiting for you to firstly recognise that it exists, and secondly, for you to activate its effectiveness in your life.

It is also a fact, that most people either just don't realise this and tend to seek this power outside of themselves or being unaware of it, just go through life struggling, by looking for answers to their challenges, obstacles, and sources of happiness from outside of themselves. What this means is that they have yet to fully embrace this inner power and in such a state, cannot shake off the mental illusions that are reinforced by society's limitations. Unless we are awakened to this limitless power of strength, wisdom and creative energy, we will continue to be burdened by fear, doubt and conditioning; that reinforce beliefs which tell us we are not capable, not worthy or not strong enough to cope.

Let me say at the outset, that awakening this power does not mean that we avoid difficulties and challenges in life, but once awakened it gives us ammunition to rise above them, knowing that absolutely no obstacle is greater than the power we have within us. Using this power to develop our inner strength, helps us to face challenges with confidence, shifts our perspective from fear to confidence; from limitation to a recognition of our unlimited potential; from being oblivious of our internal strength, to living with the profound transformative and limitless potential that is within us.

However, making that transformation requires a deep understanding that we are not separate from a greater force, the Infinite Intelligence, Universe, Source, God, or the creative energy which governs our universe. Whatever name you choose to call this force, it still means you must be awakened to the reality of the oneness or inextricable nature of this creative energy and every one of us.

The boundless power of this infinite intelligence orders the universe in perfect synchroneity and controls the mystery of nature as it produces its fruits and trees in their seasons. It regulates the vastness of the galaxy, in what can only be considered a purposeful creation. It also means being awakened to the reality that life – yours and mine - is not just a series of random happenings, but one that is deliberately created with the limitless power and potential within us. It exists to help us live our greatest lives, and not haplessly accept circumstances or let them control us. Ultimately, it means being alive to the transformational nature within us, that governs every aspect of our lives. An awareness of this means we will no longer seek power from outside of ourselves but can begin to tap into the full potential which lies within, to create happy, successful lives.

The reality of this fact is, we already have a blueprint staring us in the face! Just look around you and notice how the majestic trees standing tall and strong, stretch their branches, packed with grateful leaves and fruit, wave in the sun. And underneath these upright natural edifices, are their roots, firmly located deep into the earth's soil, extricating its goodness, as they remain unseen, silent and purposeful. These roots provide the trees with nourishing strength against the raging winds, and the changing faces of the seasons, so that they stand silently, strong and constant. Think a little further, a tree would not survive without its roots providing the strength and food for its survival but would wither and die, given the intensity of the sun and other changeable elements above the soil.

Well, you are no different. Just like the tree, within you is an unseen power or force, which when nurtured, has the potential to change your life in extra-ordinary ways. It is for this reason that I say this power is **not** external. This internal power has nothing to do with your status in society, the wealth you have, titles, or what others think about you. In fact, it certainly does not depend on your luck or good fortune, but like the roots of the tree, it exists deep within you, seeming dormant, until you choose to activate it with purpose.

This powerful force is forever present, nourishing and strengthening you, working on your behalf, although you are blissfully unaware of it. For this reason, many people feel powerless, as they struggle through life;

desperately seeking external sources for answers to their problems. Let me stress, this power existing within you, is not only real, but has been carrying you through every moment of your life thus far. Whether in good or bad times; when you rise and fall, or when you are in doubt or feel fear; this 'silent' power exists as the fountain of resilience that's been sustaining you, thus far. The good news is, once you recognise and acknowledge this force, your perspective in life begins to change – your life shifts from victimhood to you being in control; you feel much stronger, as you work to achieve your fullest potential.

As we begin, consider this book as a powerful tool, with principles and techniques that show you how to succeed in this empowerment, self-discovery journey. Additionally, this book about self-empowerment, is also about you taking responsibility for your own inner growth and happiness. By understanding the critical role and the necessity of having a **positive mindset** and **self-discipline,** you will become **aware** of the need for maintaining persistent action to create real and lasting change.

To this end, I believe that an effective strategy in achieving this aim is to be an active participant in the discovery process. It means that rather than just passively read the pages of this book, you will be actively engaged in the strategies that guide you on the path to self-discovery. Your interaction with the activities presented here will promote mastery in this shared journey. So, included in the process are practical assessments and exercises, check points and techniques, that will help you to identify and practice self-empowerment principles as a staple, into your daily life.

It is my hope that by the time you've come to the last page of this book, you will be so inspired to maximise your inner power, that the excitement and motivation to take charge of your life, will immediately begin to align with your deepest aspirations.

So, let's embark on a journey of awakening your power, as we tap into the transformational, limitless source that lies within you, together. You *will* be awakened to utilise this ever-present power, because once discovered, there is no going back! Empowerment begins with choice.

PART I:
FOUNDATIONS OF INNER AWAKENING

CHAPTER 1
UNDERSTANDING YOUR INNER POWER

What is Self-Empowerment?

So, what is self-empowerment and how do you become self-empowered? One answer may lie in the very nature of the words themselves – **self**, as well as **power.** It is to do with your nature – your own being that distinguishes you from others. At times it could be extended to your own introspection or reflexive action; what you think about yourself personally or what you do for yourself. The idea of power lies in the actions you take for your own benefit. Therefore, self-empowerment can be described here as the process of recognising and harnessing your inner strength or power, your abilities, and the potential to take control of your life. Through a journey to discover its true potential within you, self-empowerment is also about moving from a place of dependency, self-doubt, or victimhood to one of confidence, autonomy, and purpose. Self empowerment is not about waiting for external circumstances to change; it's about changing yourself from within. At its core, self-empowerment means the following:

- Believing in your ability to influence your life's direction.

- Taking ownership of your choices, actions, and outcomes.
- Cultivating a sense of purpose and aligning your life with your values.
- Developing resilience to overcome challenges and setbacks.

Indeed, self-empowerment is not a one-time event; it's **a lifelong journey**. It requires continuous effort, self-reflection, and a willingness to grow. Ultimately, the rewards are immense because the benefits range from experiencing greater happiness, fulfilment, and the ability to create the life you truly desire.

Self-empowerment also has a lot to do with inner power, which is shown through the qualities of strength, resilience and confidence that comes from within a person. It is also the mental, emotional, and spiritual energy that helps you face challenges, make decisions and achieve personal growth. That inner power is also about being connected to your true self, aligning your thoughts, beliefs and actions with your core values, and at the same time, trusting your instincts.

The source of inner power can come from various aspects of ourselves. The first is **self-awareness,** which is understanding your strengths, weaknesses, values, and goals. This in turn gives you a sense of control over your life and builds confidence and inner strength. When you are awakened to self-awareness, other aspects of yourself will come to the surface, such as **self-discipline.** This enables you to focus, persevere through difficulties and make consistent efforts toward your goals and contributes to your inner power.

In addition, **emotional resilience** helps you to develop the ability to handle stress, setbacks and emotional turmoil in a healthy way, and this strengthens your inner strength. For many their inner power is rooted in a deep sense of **spirituality or inner beliefs,** recognising that we have a connection to something greater than ourselves, whether it's through religion, mindfulness, or a personal philosophy. There are also those who maintain a **positive mindset** that allows them to remain hopeful and optimistic in difficult times, and this can enhance a person's inner power. Therefore, inner power can be seen as a combination of your mental, emotional and spiritual strength, and it comes from both your inherent qualities and the choices you make, to nurture and develop those qualities over time.

Self-awareness as the key to empowerment

One of the key elements to empowerment is self-awareness and this is amplified in the **Self-Empowerment Excellence Model (SEEM)**© that is discussed below. This is because self-employment plays a crucial role in allowing you to understand your own strengths, weaknesses, values and emotions. This understanding is the foundation for personal growth, decision-making, and taking control of your life. Therefore, it means that **self-awareness** develops empowerment in a multitude of ways.

Firstly, it helps you to **clarify your purpose and goals** by helping you to identify your true desires, your passions and aspirations. By understanding your own motivations, you can set clear and meaningful goals, and this will empower you to take proactive steps towards achieving them. Being self-aware helps you to recognise your emotional responses in different situations. In turn, this emotional intelligence allows you to manage reactions effectively, reducing impulsivity, and enhances your decision-making skills. Ultimately this enables you to become more confident, to make intentional actions to improve your life. The fact is, when you are aware of your strengths and capabilities, you are more likely to believe in yourself and take risks. Self-awareness **boosts self-esteem**, which is key to feeling empowered and capable of overcoming challenges.

Self-awareness involves an understanding of **personal values and priorities**. This enables you to make decisions that are aligned with your core beliefs. It helps you feel that you are more in control of your life and more empowered to take responsibility for your actions. In other words, it promotes **better decision-making.** Self-awareness also encourages you to **reflect on your experiences**, and to learn from them, and at the same time, to adapt where it's necessary.

This in turn **develops resilience** and the ability to bounce back from setbacks, because ultimately, it makes you more empowered to face future challenges.

In terms of **interpersonal skills**, self-awareness can improve your relationships with others. By understanding how your behaviour affects those around you, you can **communicate more effectively**, and this leads to a healthier, more supportive relationship that contribute to empowerment in social and professional contexts. In essence, self-awareness enables you to harness inner resources, it helps you to make choices that reflect your true self and build a life that aligns with your values – all of which are empowering.

Background to our *Self-Empowerment Excellence Model (SEEM)*©

Our Self-Empowerment Excellence Model (SEEM)© grew from a former excellence model that I had created as an approach to managing adverse behaviour in Secondary School (High School) pupils which resulted in their transformed self-discipline, self-awareness and positive mindset, then their enhanced academic achievement. Some 25 years ago, I was the Principal of a Tutorial College for Secondary/High School students, with its attached, Primary School and cohort of Special Education Needs pupils. During this time, our strategies for behaviour change were based on research I had conducted at the school entitled,

Managing Challenging Behaviour: A British Caribbean Perspective. This document showcased an *Excellence Model* of behaviour management which was created for the pupils of this Education Network. At that time, an excellent behaviour model, was needed to help the staff manage the pupils' adverse behaviour, which was hindering their access to the curriculum.

Embodied in this model were culturally sensitive and socially specific approaches to dealing with the children, who were displaying a variety of challenging behaviours: such as Emotional Behavioural Difficulties, (EBD), Attention Deficit Hyper-Activity Disorder (ADHD), Asperger's Syndrome, and mental health issues arising from Emotional and Social Behavioural Difficulties (EBSD), within the school.

The model worked perfectly, we achieved our goals, and it impacted on the student's ability to engage the curriculum. Many of the students were categorised as having **Special Educational Needs (SEN)** and had come to our school with their adverse records of challenging behaviours in other schools. They were disaffected students, with high levels of school exclusions and expulsions (from their previous schools), and a few were already engaging with the criminal justice system.

To deal with their challenging behaviours, I created this special Behaviour Excellence Model, using a triangular relationship between families/communities, the pupils themselves and the educational institutions responsible for their education. The effectiveness of the Model was based on the interdependence of all participants in the triangle, and it included incentivising and affecting pupil's self-esteem and confidence, as well as increasing very meaningful parental participation and insisting on a deeper collaborative input from educational stakeholders. Given the fluidity of this triangular relationship, it led to pupils' (psychologically and emotionally), engaging in a process of change, that resulted in their achievements on many levels.

Several goals and aspirations were reached by using the Behaviour Excellence Model, such as developing **self-discipline**; by helping students develop their confidence. This was achievable because of their **awareness** of a need to reflect and take control of their own actions, resulted in a positive **mindset** – both about themselves and their academic output. This had an impact on several areas of the school curriculum. For example, it helped to develop in them a more continuous devotion to learning and development. They developed a **greater sense of self-esteem and identity,** which ultimately helped them to increase their efforts and maintain stability in their set goals. Overall, the evidence showed a commitment to participatory citizenship, positive behaviour management, and general engagement in school; as well as an awareness of how this impacts their lives, in school as well as the wider society.

Now, the reason why I alluded to this previous Behaviour Excellence Model and currently draw parallels with it to gaining self-empowerment from the inner power within you, is because the principles of self-empowerment, discussed above which involved children, can also be applied to everyone; irrespective of their age, race, class, gender, religion, political and other social persuasions; in influencing behaviour change, with good measurable outcomes.

The children's Behaviour Excellence Model employed a culturally sensitive and socially specific approach to education development, which added to the high ratio of effectiveness in their successful behaviours. We were able to achieve engagement of pupils' and parents,' all at levels of the curriculum, with 90 -100% success rates.

What is interesting about the educational behaviour excellence model and its triangular relationship to the current subject of self-empowerment, is that there is a corelation in the behaviour excellence model benchmarks for students and the self-empowerment excellence model for adults, that result in transformational behaviour change to **self-discipline, awareness** and a **positive mindset**.

The fact is, **self-empowerment** was also a key element in promoting self-discipline, positive mindset and self-awareness among the children in school, which led them to succeed in a holistic way. The reason for this was the need for a self-regulatory route to behaviour change and a changed mindset. As already stated, it was effective and impacted on the pupils' mindset in promoting the longevity of self-awareness. Similarly, below, I present a triangular model to self-empowerment, to help you successfully tap into the power within you.

The Self-Empowerment Excellence Model© (SEEM)

The model presented here, and relevant for the purpose of this book, is called the **Self-Empowerment Excellence Model© SEEM**. This Model is based on the interconnection and foundation of the three key elements of Self-Empowerment, which are ***Self-discipline, Mindset and Self Awareness***. These three pillars in our triangle of interaction, require an in-depth understanding of their necessity in your life, to gain personal growth and excellence. My excitement in applying this model, with confidence in this book, is knowing, based on 30 years of experience on behaviour change, that these elements will guide you successfully to tap into, and awaken, the innate power within you.

The **Self-Empowerment Excellence Model SEEM©** is easily understood here via the diagram of a triangle, with its tripartite relationship, involving **Self-Discipline, Positive Mindset, and Self-Awareness**, as key elements of self-empowerment. This model reinforces *Best Practice* to achieving one's goals and aspirations in self-development strategies.

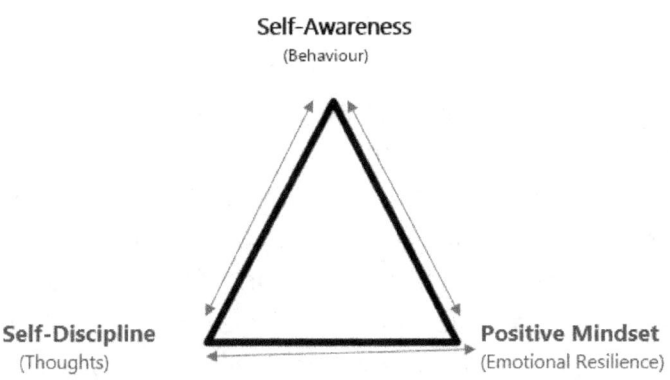

NOTE: *The SEEM© model shows Self-Awareness at the top, guiding and informing both Positive Mindset and Self-Discipline form the base, supporting as they reinforce each other.*

Self-Discipline

In looking at how this model works in relation to **Self-Empowerment and how this can awaken the power within you;** we can see that Self-discipline is positioned as one of the main foundations of the pyramid. It represents the ability to control impulses, stay focused, and consistently acts toward your goals. Without self-discipline, it's difficult to build the habits and routines that are necessary for your success. Self-discipline is the driving force that keeps you moving forward, even when your motivation wanes. Self-Discipline is not just about thinking positively; it requires deliberate action. And what does it mean to take action? Taking action involves setting clear goals, making informed decisions, and stepping out of one's comfort zone. This component emphasises the importance of initiative, persistence, and responsibility.

On a practical level, self-discipline can be developed by starting small, manageable goals. By breaking large goals into smaller, manageable steps, you can build momentum and confidence in your ability to effect changes in your life. However, you will need to create routines and stick to them. For additional support, you can use tools like habit-trackers or accountability partners, (those who can check on how you are doing), as these would help to increase your levels of motivation and help you stay on track.

Positive Mindset

Then we move to another foundational point in the triangle that is necessary to help you attain the power within you, and that is a **positive mindset**. This is the attitude and perspective you bring to the challenges and opportunities that you face. As you can see, **positive mindset** is another one of the foundations of empowerment.

It refers to the beliefs, attitudes, and perspectives that shape your approach to challenges and opportunities. A **growth mindset**, as opposed to a fixed mindset, **allows you to embrace learning, resilience, and adaptability**. By cultivating a positive and proactive mindset, you can overcome self-doubt, reframe challenges as opportunities, and remain motivated to achieve your goals.

A positive mindset also involves optimism, resilience, and the belief that you can overcome obstacles. This kind of mindset is necessary to fuel your motivation, and help you to see possibilities, rather than limitations. In this triangular relationship, it works together with self-discipline, to help keep you on track. On a practical level, a positive mindset impact self-empowerment by helping you to reframe challenges and instead, see them as opportunities for growth or change. In other words, it can help you change how you think or change how you see a set-back; for example, as an opportunity to reassess an aspect of your life. Overall, a positive mindset helps you to build resilience and reduce the impact of setbacks in your life.

Self-Awareness

At the pinnacle of the pyramid, is Self-Awareness. It involves an understanding of your strengths, weaknesses, emotions, and values. Self-awareness allows you to align your actions with your goals and make intentional choices. It also helps you recognise when adjustments are needed in your mindset or discipline. Self-awareness also involves understanding, managing, and leveraging emotions effectively. Self-awareness, emotional intelligence, and resilience play key roles in this component. Once you can master your emotions you can navigate stress, and handle setbacks with grace, and maintain focus on your goals. Developing skills such as mindfulness, stress management, and self-regulation will enable you to maintain a sense of balance and purpose in your journey toward empowerment.

How do these components above work together in real-life scenarios to create self-awareness? Well, let's imagine you are pursuing a career goal, having self-discipline ensures you will work consistently towards it. This will necessitate a positive mindset, as it will help you to stay motivated, despite receiving rejection letters or other roadblocks to your applications. Similarly, being aware of the roadblocks to self-awareness, allows you to assess your progress and adjust your approach, where relevant.

The Route to Self-empowerment

True self-empowerment is not a one-time achievement but **a continuous journey**. Sustaining growth and transformation involves lifelong learning, adaptability, and self-reflection. When you are empowered, you will set new goals, remain open to change, and consistently seek ways to improve. By embracing change and staying committed to self-development, it will ensure that your growth is both sustainable and impactful over the long term.

At the same time, you should also build meaningful relationships and networks or strong connection, as this is crucial for your empowerment. The power of connection refers to leveraging social and professional support systems, learning from others, and collaborating to achieve greater outcomes. Having strong connections with mentors, peers, and community members provide encouragement, accountability, and opportunities for growth. Once you are empowered you will recognise the value of teamwork, shared knowledge, and mutual support in achieving your success.

The discussion so far has presented the inter-relationship between a strong mindset, **(Positive mindset)** proactive action, meaningful connections, emotional intelligence, **(Self-discipline)** and a commitment to continuous development **(self-awareness)**, to achieve lasting empowerment. Overall, this **Self-Empowerment Excellence Model (SEEM),**© provides a comprehensive approach to personal and professional growth. It serves as **a roadmap** in your journey to tapping into the power within you; one that will enable you to take control of your life, overcome obstacles, and achieve your highest potential.

Inter-relationships in the Triangle

Let's look at the relationship between these key components of the triangular model in more detail. As you can see, each element plays a crucial role in contributing to the synergy of self-Empowerment as it impacts on a person in a holistic way. We will now explore further how these key components relate to each other, by creating a feedback loop that provides continuous growth and empowerment when they work together.

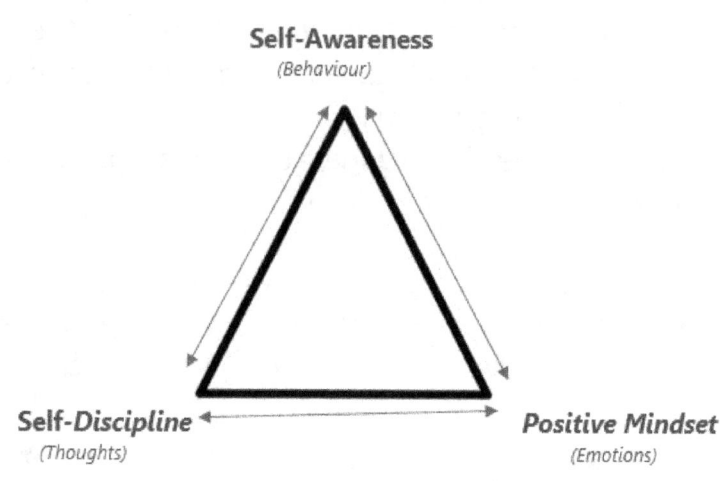

> **Self-discipline** supports **self-awareness** by creating the structure and consistency needed to reflect on your actions and behaviours. **Self-awareness** enhances **a positive mindset** by helping you identify and challenge negative thought patterns. **A positive mindset** reinforces **self-discipline** by providing the motivation and energy to stay committed to your goals.

This **Self-Empowerment Excellence Model (SEEM)©**, represented by the interconnecting points of this pyramid shows **self-discipline, positive mindset**, and **self-awareness**, (foundation pillars), to be a structured, holistic framework for transformational and personal growth. These pillars are essential for developing your self-empowerment and awakening the power within you.

The Synergy of the Model: Why It Works

The true power of this model lies in the **interconnectedness** of its components. Each element reinforces and supports the others, creating a virtuous cycle of growth and empowerment:

- **Self-discipline** provides the structure and consistency needed to develop self-awareness and maintain a positive mindset.

- **A positive mindset** fuels the motivation and resilience required to practice self-discipline and engage in self-reflection.

- **Self-awareness** ensures that your efforts are aligned with your true self, making your journey toward empowerment meaningful and sustainable.

This synergy creates a feedback loop that amplifies your growth, and as you become more disciplined, your mindset improves. In other words, when your mindset improves, you become more self-aware. And as you become more self-aware, your discipline and mindset are refined further. This cycle propels you toward greater self-empowerment and helps you awaken the power within.

Let's break down why this model is effective, transformative, and how it will benefit you.

1. SELF-DISCIPLINE: *Building the Foundation for Action*

Why it's crucial: Self-discipline is crucial because it is the bedrock of self-empowerment. Without the ability to take consistent action, even the best intentions and ideas remain unrealised. Discipline turns dreams into actionable steps and helps you stay committed to your goals, even when external motivation fades.

Self-Discipline awakens power within you. When you cultivate self-discipline, you prove to yourself that you can take control of your life. This builds confidence and a sense of agency, which are key components of self-empowerment. Over time, disciplined action becomes a habit, and you begin to trust your ability to create change.

2. POSITIVE MINDSET: *Fuelling Resilience and Possibility*

Why is having a positive Mindset crucial? A positive mindset shifts your perspective from one of limitation to one of opportunity. It helps you to see challenges as temporary and surmountable, which is essential for maintaining momentum in the face of adversity.

Positive Mindset awakens power within you because a positive mindset empowers you to believe in your potential and envisions a better future. It reduces the impact of fear, doubt, and negativity, and allows you to tap into your inner strength and creativity. When you approach life with optimism, you're more likely to take risks, learn from failures, and persist until you succeed.

3. SELF-AWARENESS: *Aligning Actions with Purpose*

Self-Awareness is crucial because it is the guiding force that ensures your actions are aligned with your values, goals, and authentic self. Without self-awareness, you may find yourself pursuing goals that don't truly resonate with you, leading to dissatisfaction and burnout.

Self-Awareness also awakens the power within you, by allowing you to understand your strengths, weaknesses, emotions, and motivations. This deep understanding helps you to make intentional choices, set meaningful goals, and live a life that feels authentic and fulfilling. It also enables you to recognize and break free from self-limiting beliefs, thereby unlocking your full potential.

The Transformative *Self-Empowerment Model of Excellence* (SEEM)©

This model is transformative because it addresses the holistic make up of self-empowered selves, which is the **mind**, **body**, and **spirit**. This transformation occurs in the following ways:

- **This model transforms the Mind:** Having a positive mindset shapes your thoughts and beliefs.

- **It also transforms the Body:** Your body is active when your self-discipline translates your thoughts into action.

- **The model also transforms the Spirit:** This is achieved because self-awareness connects your actions to your deeper purpose.

By integrating these three elements, the model helps you move from a state of **reactivity** (where life happens to you) to a state of **proactivity** (where you create the life you want). It awakens the power within, by showing you how to use tools to shape your reality - no matter which point you're starting from.

The **Self-empowerment Excellence Model (SEEM)**© is not just a theoretical framework; it's a practical guide for living a purposeful, empowered life. By cultivating self-discipline, nurturing a positive mindset, and deepening self-awareness, you can unlock your potential and step into your power. Therefore, I believe that applying the self-empowerment model of excellence - **self-discipline**, **positive mindset**, and **self-awareness** - to **awakening the power within,** is a transformative process. This process involves tapping into your inner potential, breaking free from self-limiting beliefs, and stepping into your authentic, empowered self.

Embarking on a journey toward self-empowerment begins with one crucial step: **self-awareness.** Understanding your **mindset** - the beliefs, attitudes, and thought patterns that shape how you perceive and respond to the world - is essential for meaningful growth.

In summary, the **Self-empowerment Excellence Model (SEEM)**© model reminds us that self-empowerment is not a destination but a journey - one that requires continuous effort, reflection, and growth. And what better way to achieve this, than to have clear evidence of measurable information of your current mindset, at the beginning of your journey. Later, you can then use this information to track and measure your progress, as you reflect on areas of improvement, and experience your changing growth-oriented perspective.

CHAPTER 2
AFFIRMATIONS – Beyond limitations

Before we explore the challenges and roadblocks that you have been experiencing or are likely to meet on your journey to tapping into your inner strength and power, you will be prompted to consider **affirmations** as part of your transformational strategies along your journey to self-empowerment. To understand their efficacy and how they impact on your transformation, I will firstly introduce you to the power of using affirmations in your life, generally. They are presented throughout this book as practical tools to help you overcome various challenges and roadblocks, in order to live more intentionally, as you experience a developing power and strength from within you.

⇒ **What are affirmations?**

In the fast-paced world we live in, it's easy to get overwhelmed by negativity, self-doubt, and limiting beliefs. But what if there was a simple, powerful tool that could help rewire your mindset, build confidence, and attract positivity into your life? Yes, there is such a tool it's – **affirmations!**

Affirmations are more than just words - they are declarations of intention, alignment, and transformation. When rooted in truth and spoken with conviction, affirmations help rewire the mind, disrupt limiting beliefs, and create space for new possibilities. But for affirmations to truly work, they must be supported by inner work. This is where our **Self-Empowerment Excellence Model (SEEM)**© comes in. For example, within the principles of the Model, **Self-awareness** allows you to recognize the inner narratives that have kept you small. **Self-discipline** empowers you to consistently choose thoughts and words that uplift rather than diminish. And a **positive mindset** opens the door to believe in what's possible - even before you see it. Affirmations aren't about denying reality; they're about claiming your power to move beyond old limitations and consciously create a new one.

Affirmations are used throughout this book, and though you may have heard of them in a yoga class, social media or even on TikTok, they are positive statements that you repeat to yourself to challenge and overcome self-sabotaging or negative thoughts. Think of them as mental workouts – designed to reprogramme your subconscious mind and shape the way you see yourself and your life.

These statements are often short, present-tense and are emotionally charged. Examples include, *"I am confident,"* or *"I am worthy of love and respect."* Affirmations are not just fluffy feel-good phrases. They are grounded in psychology and neuroscience. Studies have shown that positive affirmations can actually increase activity in areas of the brain that is associated with self-processing and valuation; particularly when we affirm things that matter deeply to us. Think of them as mental nutrition. If your inner critic is feeding you junk food all day – stuff like, *"I'm not good enough,"* or *"I always mess things up,"* – affirmations are your healthy intentional response. They are like saying to yourself, *"Wait a minute. I get to decide how I speak to myself."*

⇒ What do Affirmations Mean in Practice?

At their core, affirmations are about intention. They reflect what you want to believe or reinforce about yourself or your reality. Whether it's personal growth, healing, success, or peace of mind, affirmations help you align your internal narrative with your desired life experience. They are not about denying reality or pretending everything is perfect. Instead, affirmations acknowledge your power to influence your thoughts, behaviours and ultimately, your results.

⇒ Why do Affirmations matter?

Well, here's the thing; our brains love patterns. And the more we repeat something – good or bad – the more our brain accepts it as truth. Science backs this up. Studies show that affirmations can activate areas of the brain involved in self-processing and reward. So, when you repeat something like, *"I am not good enough,"* over time, your brain begins to believe it and behave accordingly. This belief then influences your actions...which influences your reality. It's a ripple effect!

Affirmations are most effective when combined with action, self-awareness and consistency. They won't magically fix everything overnight, but over time, they can shift your mental landscape, change how you perceive yourself, and influence the choices you make. When used intentionally, affirmations become more than words, they become declarations of who you are becoming. They are simple but powerful tools for transforming your mindset and empowering your journey. Whether you are looking to boost your confidence, reduce anxiety, or stay motivated, affirmations can help you cultivate a more positive, intentional inner world. You should start small, stay consistent and watch the shift to your desires unfold – one affirmation at a time.

⇒ **How do Affirmations Work?**

From a scientific perspective, because affirmations transform your mindset, they engage your thoughts and every thought carries energy. The law of attraction sets the tone for what you achieve in your life – not just wishful thinking – it's about alignment. When the mind focuses on something with clarity and intention; you naturally gravitate towards people and circumstances that resonate with similar energy. There is a sense that the mind is like a radio with a specific frequency, and you turn your life to align with that energy frequency. Consequently, the universe responds by sending you experiences that align with such frequency. For example, not as a fleeting thought or vague wish, your intention gives direction and transfers random ideas into **focused energy.** In other words, if you state, "*I'm becoming happy,*" or "*I am ready to find peace and joy in my daily life,*" with full commitment and belief, this creates a much stronger pull toward that outcome. Equally important is your ability to focus without jumping from one worry to another; focus is the fuel that powers your intention.

When you hold a clear unwavering thought in your mind, whether it is about love, success or personal growth, you begin to strengthen the connection between the inner desires and the external reality, and that is where your practice becomes very powerful. By saying a phrase repeatedly, you are anchoring your focus; it's like planting a seed in fertile soil and watering it persistently. Each repetition nurtures that thought, allowing it to grow into something tangible over time. This practice of silently repeating affirmations or phrases in your head, is deceptively simpler but incredibly powerful.

Affirmations work because your mind is wired to believe what you constantly tell it. By expressing specific goals and affirmations that align with your goals and desires, you create a mental framework that shifts your thoughts, emotions and actions, towards what you want to achieve. For example, imagine you are seeking financial abundance, a common affirmation might be, *"Money flows to me effortlessly and abundantly."* If your need is self-confidence, you might repeat, *"I am strong, capable and worthy."* And if your inner peace is what you're after, you might repeat, *"I am calm, centred and at peace with myself and the world."* The secret to making these affirmations work, is not just repetition, it's how you say them in your mind; you must feel the truth behind the words you are uttering. In other words, **your language must be emotionally charged** to impress on your subconscious mind, which obeys your script without question or evaluation, but acts according to the instructions that are given to it.

When you say, "I *am worthy of success*," you must visualise yourself succeeding; meaning, you must imagine the pride, joy and relief that comes with your success. Why is this so? It is because the emotion you attach to the affirmation, amplifies its impact, as it sends a stronger signal to your subconscious mind – the deeper layers of consciousness, where beliefs are formed and reality is literally controlled. At this point your brain operates in *theta* frequency, when you can literally reprogram limiting beliefs and install new patterns of thinking.

It's rather like your computer, when you clear the cache, it runs faster and closes unnecessary programs. That's what affirmations do for your mind; it clears the mental clutter and frees up processing power for what really matters. In this process, belief is crucial because, if you are just repeating phrases, and you don't truly believe what you are saying, then the practice loses its power. Your subconscious mind will detect the insincerity as a weak signal, with less effect. This is why starting with affirmations that seem more achievable is often more effective.

Instead of affirming, *"I have a million dollars,"* try saying, *"I am attracting opportunities that will increase my financial success."* The beauty of this technique lies in its flexibility. Another benefit to this practice is that you can express your affirmations anywhere - while commuting, during a quiet moment at work, or just before going to bed. With each repetition, you will be programming your mind to focus on what you want, rather than what you fear.

⇒ **Affirmations and Neuroscience**

Over time this repeated affirmation becomes part of your belief system, shaping how you perceive yourself and the world around you. The Reticular Activating System (or RAS) is a small but powerful part of your brain that acts like a filter for your thoughts and perceptions. It processes what you pay attention to and helps you focus on the things that matter to you most. Therefore, when you repeatedly think about a goal or desire, RAS begins to tune out irrelevant information and directs your awareness to anything that aligns with your focus. This is backed by studies conducted by Dr. Candace Pert, a neuroscientist and pharmacologist who was a pioneer in the field. Her research show emotions and thoughts affect the body at a cellular level, so that **every thought creates chemical messengers that interact with cells** throughout the body, affecting immune function, metabolism and even gene expression.

For example, if you decide to buy a particular car, and suddenly started noticing that car everywhere, that's your RAS in action. The fact is, the car was always there, but your brain just did not highlight it until you made it a significant desire. Therefore, the same principle applies to your thoughts. By saying affirmations in your head, you are training your RAS to notice opportunities, ideas and connections that bring you closer to what you desire.

Additionally, beyond the science of the RAS, lies the concept of vibrational energy. Every thought and emotion we have carries a unique frequency. Positive emotions like joy, gratitude and love, vibrate at higher frequencies, while negativity and doubt operate on lower ones. According to this principle, the universe responds to your dominant vibration, and when you admit positive energy consistently, you attract people, experiences and perform the actions that resonate with that same positivity.

For example, you can think of it like tuning a radio. If you want to hear a specific station, you must adjust the dial to the correct frequency. Your thoughts and emotions are that dial. So, if your mind is focused on abundance, gratitude and possibility, you're aligning with the station that broadcasts those outcomes into reality.

Overall, combining the RAS with the vibrational energy concept, creates a powerful feedback loop. **Your affirmations activate your RAS**, guiding you to opportunities you may have overlooked, and at the same time, the positive emotions tied to these affirmations, raise your vibrational frequency, amplifying your ability to attract what you want. These two mechanisms work together seamlessly, turning focused thoughts into tangible results.

⇒ **The Language of Affirmations**

The words you use to express your affirmations dictate their outcome. For example, it's important to be clear about your goals and frame them in a positive, but present- tense statement. For example, instead of saying, *"I want to be successful,"* which is vague and focused on lack, you need to rephrase it into something that embodies the <u>feeling of already having</u> what you want. In other words, a stronger affirmation would be, *"I'm successful and attract opportunities with ease."* This statement shifts your focus from <u>wanting</u> to already <u>having,</u> which creates a sense that you have accomplished what you want; so, this attracts the energy of success.

When creating affirmations, use specific and powerful language. For example, if you're working on your health, instead of just saying, *"I'm healthy,"* you could try repeating something like, *"I'm full of vibrant health and my body is strong and energised, every day."* This statement not only focuses on physical health, but it also emphasises vitality and energy, which are more **emotionally engaging.**

In recent years, modern neuroscience has illuminated the **powerful ability of the human brain to reshape itself** in response to focused mental exercises. According to Dr. Doidge, a psychiatrist, psychoanalyst and expert on the subject, this process is known as neuroplasticity. He states that the structure and function of your brain are not fixed, but malleable, capable of being transformed by your thoughts, emotions and behaviours. Accordingly, he confirms that the brain is able to form new neural connections, when we repetitively affirm. This plays a vital role in learning, healing and personal development. In other words, it is important to include words in your affirmations that resonate with you emotionally, so that the more connected you feel to the affirmation, the more powerful the results of your corresponding actions will be.

⇒ **When do I practice Affirmations?**

The best times to practice affirmations are when your mind is most receptive, which typically happens during moments of stillness. Examples are the first thing in the morning, or right after waking up. This is an ideal time because your subconscious mind is more open before the day's distractions take over. Another powerful moment is just before going to sleep because the brain is in a relaxed pre-dream state, which allows your affirmations to sink in deeply.

If you practice during these times, it's easier to bypass any negative thoughts or doubts that might arise during the day. However, having said that, based on your personal or unique circumstances, you don't have to limit yourself to just these times during the day; any moment when you feel centred, calm and focused, is perfect for practising your affirmations. It could be during a quiet walk, while meditating or even when taking a break at work. **The key is consistency.**

⇒ **Visualisation and Affirmations**

Making affirmations a daily habit, integrating them into the flow of your day and repeating them when your mind is in a state of openness, enhances the power of your affirmations, combined with visualisation. When you mentally repeat your affirmations, you can close your eyes and imagine yourself already living the outcome you desire. Visualise yourself in the situations experiencing the feelings and focus on the sights and sounds that are associated with your success. The fact is, the more vividly you can imagine it, the stronger the emotional connection will be to your affirmation. This type of visualisation makes the affirmation feel very real to your subconscious mind.

Visualisation adds another layer of effectiveness because it **helps your brain *see* the goal as something achievable.** When you visualise, your brain doesn't distinguish between what's real and vividly imagined experiences – meaning, your brain will accept the scenario as if it's already happening. At the same time, this creates a sense of familiarity with your desired outcome and makes it easier to attract those circumstances into your life. Dr. Joe Dispenza, Author of *Breaking the Habit of Being Yourself* confirms this principle by stating that, *"Visualisation works because neurons interpret imagery as equivalent to real action."*

Therefore, practising affirmations regularly, and combining them with powerful visualisation techniques, can deepen your connections to what you desire. Then over time, this practice will strengthen your mindset and make it easier to achieve your desires. As you continue with this practice of affirming your desires, you must pay attention to the subtle shifts in your mindset, your emotions, and even opportunities that begin to appear in your life.

However, an important reminder is that **patience and consistency are keys to a changed mindset.** It doesn't happen overnight but with dedication to the practice of expressing your affirmations, the stronger the connection will be to the changes you visualise;

your thoughts will begin to align with the reality you desire, and soon you will notice that the shifts you've been waiting for will manifest. So, as your self-awareness develops, and you become more mindful of the process of transformation taking place in your life, you will begin to identify roadblocks that have been keeping you stuck.

CHAPTER 3
ROADBLOCKS – RELEASING WHAT KEEPS YOU SMALL

Roadblocks, as the name implies, are barriers or obstacles, that can take you off your path, slows you down or hinders your progress. Literally, this can be a barricade on the road that is used to block traffic for a reason. However, metaphorically, we can use the word 'roadblock' to describe a person encountering a situation that makes it difficult or impossible for them to do what they want to do. So, in the case of the driver, her choices might be, having stopped at the roadblock, to either go back to where she came from, or use a different route. In another context, a 'roadblock' can be said to be a situation that prevents you from achieving your life's goals, whether you are aware of this or not.

Therefore, identifying roadblocks in your life is essential, so that once they are recognised, you can take the relevant steps to quickly overcome them and move forward in your life. When we set out to climb the stairs to personal growth, there is usually a tendency for roadblocks to appear in our journey as challenges or hindrances in our way. Roadblocks tend to show up in life in different ways, and we must consciously and intentionally remove them, in order to progress.

Here are some very common roadblocks to look out for; together with strategies and solutions to help you identify and manage them. One of the problems with roadblocks is that they tend to embody our personalities, our characteristics and our habits, and operate as if they are permanent features of life that we sometimes tend to believe are just a part of life that we must accept. However, as we examine their stifling effect and reveal them as hindrances to our progress and inner strength, you will begin to feel liberated, as you awaken to the power that lies within you, to consciously reject and eradicate them.

Applying the **Self-Empowerment Excellence Model (SEEM)**© which is rooted in self-discipline, self-awareness, and a positive mindset, shows that it offers a powerful framework for dismantling the roadblocks to personal growth. **Self-discipline** equips individuals to push through procrastination, perfectionism, and lack of focus, replacing scattered effort with consistent action. **Self-awareness** sheds light on hidden influences - such as limiting beliefs, childhood conditioning, and unresolved past issues, making it possible to address their root causes rather than just their symptoms. A **positive mindset** transforms the emotional terrain, reframing failure, negative thought patterns, and societal pressures into opportunities for learning and resilience. Together, these three pillars not only clear the path up the "stairs" of growth but also provide the strength, clarity, and optimism needed to keep climbing - turning obstacles into stepping stones toward lasting personal excellence.

"Climbing the Stairs to Personal Growth"

Each step represents a challenge to overcome on the journey to success and self-fulfilment. This journey to personal growth is often pictured as a staircase but for many, the steps are blocked by heavy obstacles that make the climb feel impossible. These barriers can take many forms: the sting of failure, a lack of self-confidence, chronic procrastination, and the mental weight of negative thought patterns. Without clear goals or direction, it's easy to stumble into toxic relationships, become trapped in perfectionism, or be held back by limiting beliefs. Overwhelm and burnout steal energy, while the absence of support or resources leaves one feeling alone on the climb. Unresolved past issues, weak discipline or focus, early childhood conditioning, and the pressure of societal norms or self-image, can all cement us in place. Yet each of these challenges, once recognized, can be addressed - transforming the staircase from a daunting wall into a path toward fulfilment and purpose.

1. Fear of Failure
2. Lack of Self-Confidence
3. Procrastination
4. Negative Thought Patterns
5. Lack of Goals/Direction
6. Toxic Relationships
7. Perfectionism
8. Limiting Beliefs
9. Overwhelm/Burnout
10. Lack of Support/Resources
11. Unresolved Past Issues
12. Lack of Discipline/Focus
13. Childhood Conditioning
14. Social Norms/Self-Image

Picture credit: Freepik

At the top of the stairs: **Personal Growth, Success, and Self-Empowerment!**

FEAR OF FAILURE - *ROADBLOCK*

Let's begin with a simple fact - you want to make changes in your life – and want to become more empowered, by learning how to access and utilise the power within you.

Applying the **Self-Empowerment Excellence Model (SEEM)**© to the fear of failure roadblocks, highlight the importance of practising **Self-discipline**, as you recognise the many guises that the fear of failure adopts. Then, having become aware of its debilitating effect in your life, and **reflecting** on the actions you should adopt to overcome them, the result is you will begin to experience a changed **mindset**. This change takes place as follows – you move from a position of fear, to learning how to deal and sustain positivity within you. Then you learn how to positively apply the solutions. Such a **positive mindset** reinforces your practice of self-discipline, and this begins to provide the motivation and energy you need to remain committed to your goals. The synergy from this triangular model amplifies your growth, and as you become more disciplined, your **mindset** improves. Consequently, the repetitive element of the triangle creates a cycle or loop that pushes you towards greater **self-awareness** and as a result, transformation is achieved from the **solutions,** enabling you to awaken the strength and power within you.

◊ **Self-Doubt**

A very typical roadblock generated by the fear of failure, and perhaps one of the most common, is self-doubt. This roadblock tends to show up especially when you are faced with new opportunities. It is possible that this self-doubt could have its roots in having failed before, with disastrous consequences, or due to the fear of being ridiculed by friends, who might think you are weak, not *"cool"* or just incompetent.

◊ **External Disapproval**

Indeed, you may fear that your partner might see you as being competitive and therefore you feel that doing something for yourself might upset the balance in your relationship. Additionally, it may stem from fear of being seen by extended family members as not as good as your cousin, brother, sister, or other successful family member. Moreover, fearing the, *"I told you so!"* from friends or colleagues, is a deep-seated roadblock that instils fear of trying out a new opportunity, to avoiding derision from anyone in your circle of relationships. This is burdensome and tends to break your will, as well as the courage to begin doing anything that is new.

◊ **Reflections**

Reflect on situations where you hesitate to take risks or where you avoid doing something because you're afraid of failing. The fear of failure often leads to staying in your comfort zone. It also means limiting your potential to grow and develop as a person, because your thoughts are the ropes which are anchoring you to ground level in your life.

FEAR OF FAILURE – *SOLUTIONS*

⇒ **Reframe your perspective of Failure**

There are many solutions to dealing with the fear of failure. You can begin by reframing how you view the word *"failure,"* usually as something negative and instead, see it as a learning opportunity. You can see it as an experience that teaches you where you've gone wrong, and on reflection, can offer perspectives on how you can improve on past situations. In other words, feel the fear and do whatever it is you want to do, anyway!

But how does that work, in reality? Well, you can challenge yourself by taking small risks and embracing your mistakes as part of your personal growth. In other words, increase your level of *"Do it now!"* by taking a mini step forward at a time, and whatever the outcome is, it will be a learning experience.

⇒ **Don't Broadcast your Plans!**

A wise person once told me, *"Do not broadcast your plans in advance!"* Having experienced the difference between telling others in advance and keeping information to myself until my plan came to fruition, I must emphasise that I do agree with such words of wisdom. If you are working for yourself, then it is not necessary to publicise what you are going to do. This can be a sure way to attract negativity from others for different reasons. This can range from creating self-doubt, or dampening your initial interest and belief that you *can* do what you have planned.

⇒ **Destroy the "What-ifs"**

Another solution is to work quietly on your own intuition and chosen initiatives. By doing this, you will be able to short-circuit the energy you usually devote to *"what ifs,"* and *"what will they think!"* At the same time, it will give you time and space to experience the outcome first-hand and decide how you feel about it. Afterwards, you can decide whether to make it public or not – it's entirely your choice! Doing so will give you more chances to explore opportunities to improve yourself, either by celebrating your successes with others, or just expanding your horizons privately, as you begin to embrace new experiences with more self-confidence.

Affirmations to help you deal with the Fear of Failure

Here are **Inner Shift Affirmations, Reflections and Journal Prompts,** as well as a daily **Embodiment Action**, to help you overcome the fear of failure roadblocks.

⇒ **Affirmations:**

1. "I am learning and growing through every experience, success or setback."
2. "Mistakes are stepping stones on the path to mastery."
3. "I am brave enough to try, even if I might fail."
4. "My worth is not defined by outcomes but by effort and intention."
5. "Every failure brings me one step closer to success."

⇒ **Journal Prompts:**

1. When was the last time I avoided something out of fear of failing?
2. What does failure actually mean to me?
3. How could my life shift, if I redefined failure as feedback?

Journalling, the act of writing down thoughts, according to Dr. James Pennebaker, helps to externalise your thoughts, making them easier to analyse and change.

⇒ **Embodiment Action:**

Do one small thing you've been avoiding due to fear. Write down how it felt.

Finally, I have included the above practical tools as affirmations, a guided journal prompt and reflection practice, to help you deal with an inner shift of these roadblocks. The idea is not to just *read* affirmations but to *embody* them through writing, self-inquiry and reflection.

LACK OF SELF-CONFIDENCE – *ROADBLOCK*

Another obstacle to your self-development and confidence in trying something new is low self-confidence, or a total lack of self-confidence. Low self-confidence may have its roots in different sources; even beginning from childhood, and this is explored in some detail, later in this chapter.

Let's apply the **Self-Empowerment Excellence Model (SEEM)**[c] to the lack of self-confidence roadblock. You must understand the devastating impact that negative self-talk and low confidence has on your self-esteem. Without a doubt the importance of practising **Self-discipline** in learning how to counteract this roadblock is a top priority in awakening the power within you. Then, becoming aware of the negative effect of low confidence or lack of self-confidence, and **reflecting** on the actions necessary to overcome them, the result is that your **mindset** is bound to change. This transformation moves from lacking self-confidence to learning how to sustain positivity in your life, as you learn how to apply the **solutions.** The result is your attitude will change from being negative, to a **positive mindset.** This process then begins to provide the motivation and energy you need to remain committed to your goals. It also confirms there is a synergy from this triangular model that amplifies your growth.

Consequently, the repetitive element of applying the triangle creates a loop that pushes you towards greater **self-awareness,** as you begin to understand the power that lies within you.

◊ Negative Self-talk & Feeling Unworthy

Lack of self-confidence as a roadblock is immediately noticeable from the signs which sometimes manifest as negative self-talk, feeling unworthy of success, or doubting your abilities. Ask yourself, where has such feelings come from? In fact, consider how far back in time they may have taken hold of your subconscious, causing you to self-talk negatively, or minimise what you've achieved. Low self-confidence may cause you to hide your achievements, embarrassed that others might find out about your past successes. The question is what, or who is responsible for such downplaying of your skills and abilities? This would have had a devastating impact on your psyche, so that you refuse to project yourself as someone who has dynamism or the potential to do great things.

◊ Being Put Down & Belittled Infront of Others

Sometimes the signs showing a lack of self-confidence may stem from being put down when you were a child, being belittled in the company of others, or persistently told you are not capable or good at doing things. For example, a child who is constantly praised for their efforts, rather than just their achievements, learns that their value is intrinsic and not dependent on external validation. On the other hand, a child who is frequently told they are, "*not good enough*" or has been consistently compared to others, may internalise these negative messages, and this could lead to feelings of inadequacy and a lack of self-confidence.

◊ **Reflections**

Here's how to identify this roadblock. You must pay attention to moments when you downplay your accomplishments or hold back from pursuing your goals because you don't believe in yourself, or that you can succeed in a planned project. Be conscious of how effortlessly and readily you may make excuses for disregarding your skills and abilities, whilst working with others, even when they have witnessed this themselves. This may be when someone praises you for your skills and abilities, or success, and rather than acknowledge their compliment, you dismiss it as not being important, or you don't respond to it, as if it is no consequence. It could mean that you are probably not used to positive conditioning and have grown to deny automatically, that you even have abilities! Nevertheless, it is a debilitating roadblock, and you need to break this chain of command!

LACK OF SELF-CONFIDENCE – *SOLUTIONS*

⇒ **Focus on Past Successes**

One way to deal with lack of self-confidence is to focus on past successes and reinforce in your mind, that it is **you** who have accomplished them. In fact, you may even have evidence in some form; either written, audio or other recorded evidence, of your past success. You need to purposely go and find them and when you do, begin to examine them. As you touch and feel them, imagine the thoughts behind those who created them. Imagine the pride they may have felt when they decided to award you the accolade(s). Remember, it is because they believed in your ability, and have publicised it, for the world to see and know about your achievement, as evidence for now and in your future. This then suggests that there is a potential of you repeating or replicating such success again and again.

⇒ **Set Achievable Goals**

So, with the reality of such concrete evidence, you must now set new achievable goals, and practice **self-affirmations,** to help you reframe your past conditioning. In this way you can over-ride the old conditioning, and instead internalise or reprint on your subconscious, a new set of instructions that will create new possibilities, in your present and future life.

⇒ **Mental Transformation**

Here are a few affirmations to help with your mental transformation. Say them daily to strengthen their effect. As discussed above, research shows that mindfulness practices such as repeating affirmations, enhances neuroplasticity – increasing your brain's ability to form new neural pathways. This is not about bypassing difficult emotions or maintaining fake positivity, it's about becoming the person who can authentically achieve your desires through conscious actions. Therefore, here are **Affirmations** together with an **Inner Shift Journal Prompts,** and daily **Embodiment Actions**, to help you delve deeper and strengthen your transformational journey.

Affirmations for Self-confidence

1. "My past does not define me; I rise above negativity."
2. "I trust in my abilities to overcome challenges."
3. "My inner dialogue is filled with love and encouragement."
4. "I embrace my strength and grow from my challenges."
5. "I radiate quiet strength and inner power."
6. I believe in myself more each day."

Journal Prompts:

1. What's one thing I'm good at that I often downplay?
2. Where in my life could I show up more fully?
3. How would I treat myself if I were my biggest cheerleader?

Embodiment Action:

Today you will attempt to speak up in a small way. This could be done by email, a comment, or suggesting an idea - and make a note of how it feels.

Moreover, you should surround yourself with people who are supportive of your goals; those who can reinforce your good qualities and act as confirmers of your new affirmations. Those supportive people will become a catalyst for your advancement and positive mindset. They will also act as your *"live"* influencers when you are experiencing a dip in confidence or have a *'down'* day. Additionally, they will be the ones who will lift your spirits and route for you in your race to succeed. Having a combined mindset means they will encourage you to carry on, no matter what! And that is one way to break the cycle of this very common roadblock.

PROCRASTINATION – *ROADBLOCK*

There is no doubt that we are all guilty of procrastinating sometime in our lives. If we could postpone things, so we don't have to tackle them, or use the excuse of *"I can do that later,"* or *"Does it have to be now?"* most of us would get away without having to do much. The only thing is, the tasks catch up with us, and rather than doing them in their due time, we are later forced to do them under pressure, with some measure of frustration, anger or even anxiety that this may cause; it is not worth procrastinating at all!

My grandmother used to say, *"Procrastination is the thief of time!"* When young I thought it was a Biblical reference, being the devout Christian that she was. However, later, in my academic sojourn, I learned that it is also a proverbial saying from *Night Thoughts* (1742-5) by the English poet and dramatist Edward Young. Well, I was not too surprised because she was a very clever woman, who instilled in me, at a very young age, the persistent practice of *"Do it now!"*

◊ **Practical Prevention Examples**

Generally, procrastination means putting off what you should or could do now and leaving it for later. It boils down to the fact that someone who continually puts things off will ultimately achieve little. So, I can say that I was fortunate to have had my grandmother's inspiring wisdom, as the person who influenced my early life, having been brought up by her. In fact, from as early as the age of 5, she made me recite poetry, which later graduated into making me write poems and memorise speeches or giving impromptu ones, as some *"Do it now!"* activities, to prevent boredom and what the elder women in the community called, *"Idle hands"* alluding to that state as being as precursor to involvement in *"the devil's workshop!"*

Later, when her eyesight began to fail, my daily chores included reading to her. As I grew older, I realised that doing these things had multiple benefits. Apart from her cultural beliefs about being idle, she was preparing me for future leadership positions. She remarked on the need to be what she called *"fronting jobs,"* meaning, always taking a leading position in my career. The little jobs she used to give me were scheduled as part of a routine, so there was no opportunity to procrastinate. The regularity of my activities and the punctuality which governed them, meant that there was no room to put things off. On reflection, the timeless habits she instilled in me continue to this day.

◊ **Applying the Self-Empowerment Excellence Model (SEEM)©**

Therefore, one of the first step in overcoming procrastination as a roadblock, is to apply my **Self-Empowerment Excellence Model (SEEM)©** because mind transformation is a priority in eradicating the habits and excuses that cause us to continually put off doing things that we plan to do but avoid doing. Stage one in the process is firstly to agree that developing **Self-discipline** is an important practice to break the habits of procrastination, because this is a crucial step in awakening the power within you. Moreover, becoming aware of the negative effect of procrastination and **reflecting** on the actions necessary to overcome them, will result in your changed **mindset.** This means that the transformation moves from putting things off and finding excuses for not doing what is planned, to actions that you take, as suggested in the **solutions** given for dealing with procrastination.

Applying the **Self-Empowerment Excellence Model (SEEM)**© shows that your attitude will change from being negative to a **positive mindset.** Committing to the process then begins to provide the motivation and energy you need to stick to your goals. The triangular relationship of the model also confirms that its synergy will amplify and develop your inner growth. Ultimately, the entire experience pushes you towards greater **self-awareness,** of recognition of the undisputed power that you already possess; in order to improve your life.

◊ **Reflections**

So how will you recognise the signs of procrastination? They will be the times when you consistently delay important tasks, or when you deliberately find distractions or put off making decisions, instead of doing what you should do. This could be wanting to make an unplanned cup of tea or coffee, scrolling without stopping in your social media feeds, or constantly checking your phone for messages – even reading the old ones! In addition, you will notice when you delay starting a project or when you often find yourself overwhelmed by tasks that you avoid doing.

PROCRASTINATION – *SOLUTIONS*

⇒ **Identify Underlying reasons**

We can all agree that procrastination is a common challenge that many people face, but overcoming it often requires a deeper understanding of its roots and learning practical strategies to tackle it. One effective way of breaking the cycle of procrastination is to **identify the underlying reasons** for it. For some, procrastination is tied to perfectionism or fear of failure, which can create a sense of paralysis. In these cases, shifting the focus from achieving a perfect result to simply making progress can help reduce the pressure. Embracing the idea that it's better to complete a task imperfectly than to not start at all, can make the process less daunting and more manageable.

⇒ **Break Down Tasks**

Another key approach is to break down tasks into smaller, more manageable steps. Large, overwhelming projects often lead to procrastination because the sheer scale of the task feels insurmountable. By **dividing tasks into smaller chunks**, each part becomes less intimidating, and this can make it easier to start. Additionally, setting clear deadlines for each of these mini tasks can create a sense of urgency and help maintain momentum. This is especially true when you pair this with a sense of accountability, whether it's through sharing your progress with a friend or colleague or using a productivity tool to track your work.

⇒ **Emotional & Mental Barriers**

One important aspect of overcoming procrastination involves **addressing the emotional and mental barriers** that accompany it. Often, procrastination is a form of avoidance because a task triggers negative emotions, whether it's boredom, anxiety, or frustration. To combat this, it's useful to reframe the task in a more positive light. For example, focusing on how completing the task will lead to a sense of relief or achievement can be a strong motivator. Incorporating short, scheduled breaks can also help maintain focus and prevent burnout, allowing you to refresh your mind before continuing with the work.

⇒ **Time Management Techniques**

Another strategy that can combat procrastination is the use of time management techniques, where you work for short bursts of time – typically 25 minutes – followed by a short break. This structure can **help to create a sense of urgency** and provide you with a clear path forward, without feeling overwhelmed. Additionally, removing distractions is crucial. You should set up an environment that is conducive to focused work. For example, turning off notifications or finding a quiet space, allows you to give your full attention to the task at hand. Here are a few affirmations to help your mental transformation. Say them daily to affect transformation. Research shows that mindfulness practices, such as repeating affirmations, enhances neuroplasticity – which is your brain's ability to form new neural pathways and create a new way of thinking.

⇒ **Silence Anxiety**

You can **silence the voice of anxiety** through repetition of these affirmations. Over time, this practice can reveal the subtle layers of your thoughts and emotions, offering insights into your inner experience and nurturing a compassionate presence in your everyday life.

Affirmations to help you overcome procrastination

1. "Today I take small steps."
2. "I choose action over hesitation."
3. "I release the need for perfect timing."
4. "I start now, even if it's messy."
5. Momentum builds when I begin."

Journal Prompts:

1. What task am I avoiding right now?
2. What fear or belief is tied to that avoidance?
3. What's one tiny step I can take today?

Embodiment Action:
Start the task you've been avoiding for 5 minutes. Reflect on how that shifted your mindset.

Ultimately, overcoming procrastination requires a combination of understanding the root causes, restructuring your tasks, and creating an environment that supports focused work. It takes practice and persistence, but with consistent effort, it's possible to break free from procrastination and regain control over your time and productivity.

NEGATIVE THOUGHT PATTERNS – *ROADBLOCK*

Of all the multitude of roadblocks we can be faced with, perhaps none is more extensive and pervasive as a very long list of negative thought patterns. Negative thought patterns are recurring, automatic thoughts that often focus on the worst-case scenarios, self-criticism, or distortions of reality. These thought patterns, such as overthinking, or criticising, can significantly impact mental health, leading to feelings of anxiety, sadness or low self-esteem. Recognising and understanding these patterns is the first step in breaking the cycle, as they can often lead to unproductive behaviours and hinder your personal growth. By addressing these patterns, you can develop healthier thinking habits and improve your overall well-being.

So, what are the signs of negative thought patterns? Let's begin with a thought pattern that has you persistently criticising your abilities or overthinking by focusing on worst-case scenarios. Once you identify this trait, you should be mindful of how often they recur, because they limit your potential and create unnecessary anxiety. Recognising negative thought patterns can be crucial for mental health and well-being. Negative thought patterns can be catastrophic. It's the times when you tend to expect the worst possible outcome or viewing situations as far worse than they are. For example, thinking, *"If I make a mistake at work, I'll get fired."* Other signs to look for are to do with over-generalisation, which is making broad conclusions based on a single event. For instance, thinking, *"I failed this test, so I'm terrible at everything."*

⇒ **Negative Self-talk**

Firstly, negative thought patterns tend to produce **negative self-talk,** and this impacts a person's self-esteem and confidence. To overcome this roadblock, it is important to apply the **Self-Empowerment Excellence Model (SEEM),** © as well as the solutions suggested below, before changes can be made. The importance of practising **Self-discipline** as you learn how to counteract this roadblock, is a top priority in tapping into the power within you. The fact is, as you become aware of the negative thought patterns, and **reflect** on the actions necessary to overcome them, the result is that your **mindset** will begin to change.

⇒ **Awareness**

Therefore, this transformation moves from lacking self-confidence to learning how to sustain positivity in your life, as you learn how to apply the **solutions.** The result is your attitude will change from being negative to a **positive mindset.** This process then begins to provide the motivation and energy that will be needed as you commit to your goals. The process of transformation confirms a synergy within this triangular model, and this will amplify your growth. Ultimately, this triangular model works in your life to create a loop that pushes you towards greater **self-awareness,** and reveals your internal power, and how this power can be utilised for your benefit.

⇒ **Reflections**

Negative thought patterns can be reflected in how you see things; sometimes as being either black or white, and with no grey area in between. In other words, it is judging situations as either all good or all bad, with no middle ground. For example, thinking, *"If I'm not perfect, I'm a failure."* In addition, negative thought patterns can be presented in over self-criticism. It is those times when you might be overly harsh or critical of yourself, often with unrealistic standards. For example, you might be plagued with self-criticism, constantly telling yourself, *"I'm not good enough,"* or *"I should be better."*

⇒ **Filtering**

Another common negative thought pattern is assuming you know what others are thinking; in other words, you become an obsessive 'mind-reader.' Such thoughts can border on assuming, *"They didn't respond to my text, so they must be upset with me."* Focusing only on the negative aspects of a situation and ignoring any positive ones is a form of filtering. In other words, it means you choose to select certain information and persistently dwell on it. An example is, *"I got one piece of feedback on my report, and it was negative – everything else doesn't matter."*

The fact that negative thought patterns overlap, if you are plagued by them, you will recognise that in addition to the above, your emotional reasoning will cause you to believe that your emotions reflect objective reality. For example, thinking, *"I feel anxious, so there must be something wrong."* This could be followed with constantly revisiting past mistakes or failures, and imagining what you could have done differently, which can lead to feeling guilty or ashamed. Worse still, is that you may discount any positive feedback or experiences. For example, thinking, *"They only complimented me because they have to; it doesn't mean anything."* If you notice any of the above thought patterns, it might help to take a step back and challenge your thoughts. Ask yourself if they are based on evidence, or you can reframe them in a more balanced way.

NEGATIVE THOUGHT PATTERNS – *SOLUTIONS*

There are several practical steps you can take to deal with negative thought patterns and improve your mental well-being. There are many effective strategies and some of them are presented below.

⇒ You can **practice Self-Awareness** by observing your thoughts. Start by paying attention to your thoughts. Try to notice when you are slipping into negative thinking or when a pattern begins to emerge.

⇒ A practical way of dealing with negative thought patterns is through **Journaling.** Writing down your thoughts can help you become more aware of them and give you the space to reflect on whether they're based on reality.

⇒ Another alternative is to **seek professional help** – Cognitive behavioural therapy (CBT) is one approach that can be particularly effective in addressing these kinds of negative thought patterns.

⇒ Furthermore, you can **challenge your thoughts**. Ask yourself questions or question the evidence, *"What's the evidence for this* thought? *Is it based on facts or assumptions?"* For example, if you're thinking, *"I'm terrible at this,"* ask yourself to recall moments when you did succeed.

⇒ Another thing you can do is to **look for alternatives.** Try to identify other possible explanations or perspectives. For example, instead of thinking, *"I'm a failure,"* consider, *"I made a mistake, but I can learn from this."*

⇒ You can also try to replace the negative thoughts with more balanced ones. It is called **reframing your negative thoughts**. This might be easier said than done but here is an example. Instead of thinking, *"This is too hard, I can't do it,"* reframe it to, *"This is challenging, but I can break it down into manageable steps."* You must also focus on the positive. Even if something didn't go as planned, try to find something positive to take from the experience, no matter how small.

⇒ The practice of **Mindfulness meditation** is another good way to help you become more aware of your thoughts and feelings without judging them. By learning to observe your thoughts, without becoming attached to them, you can break the cycle of negative thinking. There are many grounding exercises where you focus on your senses to anchor yourself in the present moment, to reduce over-thinking and rumination.

⇒ Using positive affirmations helps to counter self-criticism. **Engaging in positive Self Talk**, is one way to recreate a positive thought pattern. Here are examples of Affirmations for Positive Self Talk to help you on your self-empowerment journey as follows:
   1. *"I challenge my thoughts with kindness."*
   2. *"My mind is a garden; I plant empowerment."*
   3. *"I choose thoughts that support me."*
   4. *"I observe and shift my inner dialogue."*
   5. *"I am the master of my mindset."*

⇒ Repeating this often can help to reinforce a positive thought pattern. Another very important strategy of removing negative thought pattern is being **kind to yourself**. Treat yourself as you would treat a friend. If a friend was struggling, you would want to offer encouragement, instead of harsh criticism to them. Seeing yourself as someone who is worthy of kindness, adds worth or value to how you treat yourself.

⇒ Putting in effort brings results. If you catch yourself dwelling on negative thoughts, you should do all you can to **break this cycle of rumination**. This you can do by shifting your focus onto something else. This can be taking up a hobby, talking to a friend or going for a walk. If you find it difficult to make a big change in your thought pattern, why not **set a time limit**, on the time spent on a negative thought? For example, you can set 10 minutes as a limit to think about it, then purposely move on to something else. This way you will be taking control and not letting your unruly thoughts dominate or control what you think, or how long you hold on to those thoughts.

⇒ As with all things, when we are making great changes, we need to challenge unrealistic or perfectionist expectations. You should recognise that no one is perfect, and mistakes are a normal part of learning and growing. Therefore, you should **set realistic expectations,** and at the same time you should not be afraid to **celebrate the small wins or successes**. This can help shift your focus from what is going wrong to what is going right.

⇒ We each have different coping strategies in coping with difficulties, but an overall advice must be to choose strategies to significantly reduce things like **physical activity**, to relieve stress and anxiety and improve your mood. At the same time, you need to **develop relaxation**

techniques by practicing deep breathing, yoga or progressive muscle relaxation. This helps you to manage stress and anxiety, which are often culprits that fuel negative thinking. If you find it difficult at any point along the way, in conquering your negative thought patterns, another alternative is to **seek professional support**.

Cognitive Behaviour Therapy (CBT) is particularly effective in helping people challenge and change negative thought patterns. A Therapist can help you learn strategies to reframe and reduce unhelpful thoughts. Additionally, talking with others or joining a Support Group, with those who have similar experiences, can help you feel less isolated in your struggles.

⇒ How can you make those changes last? A very good friend of mine suggested that in trying to maintain the changes to your negative thought pattern, you will need to **build resilience.** Resilience can be built by **practising self-compassion**, which means being patient with yourself as you work through negative thought patterns. The fact is, it is normal to have setbacks, but with consistent practice, it will become easier to change the way you think. In addition to the suggestions above, a very important way of maintaining and experiencing longevity of your changes, is to also practise **expressing gratitude**. Take time each day to **reflect on things you are thankful for**. This simple practice can shift your focus from what is wrong, to what is going well in your life, and increases your excitement and interest in what will come next.

Here is a **Journal prompt** and **Embodiment Action** to help deepen your inner shift from negative thought patterns as you make progress in your transformational journey.

Journal Prompts:

1. What thought patterns show up often and hold me back?
2. How do those thoughts sound - like someone else's voice?
3. What new thought can I replace them with?

Embodiment Action:
Write down one recurring negative thought and reframe it with an affirmation.

In summary, recognising negative thought patterns is the first step. Once you are aware of them, challenging and reframing those thoughts, **practising mindfulness,** and engaging in healthy coping strategies, can help shift your mindset. **Being consistent with these practices** over time, can lead to lasting changes in how you think and feel. Therefore, you should now begin to understand that in this early stage of your journey, to discover your power within, is also one of self-realisation; about being honest with what you discover about yourself and where you are at present in the journey. This promotes clarity of purpose and helps you to embrace the actions (**self-discipline**) that are necessary to achieve your desires and at the same time, make lasting changes in your life, (**positive mindset**).

LACK OF CLEAR GOALS/DIRECTION – *ROADBLOCK*

We now move on to another area that is equally as debilitating as negative thought patterns, and that is **lacking clear goals or directions to move forward**. You will discover, as we explore this condition, that lacking clear goals, and negative thought patterns, are both significant roadblocks to feeling empowered. In fact, they often overlap, by working together to limit your potential. While negative thoughts can create self-doubt and a sense of inadequacy, **the absence of clear goals** amplifies this feeling, by making it difficult to focus on specific achievements or direction.

The fact is, when you are trapped in a cycle of negativity, you may find it even harder to define what you want or set meaningful objectives. Conversely, without clear goals to guide your efforts, you may become more susceptible to negative thinking, because you feel uncertain about your progress or direction. Together, these obstacles create a cycle that prevents you from taking proactive steps and ultimately, they hinder your ability to feel empowered or be in control of your life.

Lacking clear goals or direction can significantly undermine your sense of empowerment. When you are unsure of what you want to achieve or where you are headed, you often feel lost, disconnected and unsure of your capabilities. Without clear objectives, it becomes difficult to measure progress or celebrate small wins, which can lead to feelings of helplessness or frustration. A lack of direction also hampers decision-making, as there is no clear framework or purpose to guide your choices. This uncertainty erodes confidence, making it harder for you to take initiative or pursue opportunities. Ultimately, the absence of clear goals leaves you feeling disempowered, as you struggle to harness their energy and efforts toward meaningful action.

How many times have you felt lost, directionless or uncertain about what you want out of life? If you often feel unmotivated or unsure of what steps to take next, it may be because you don't have a clear vision of what you want to achieve. The signs of lacking clear goals can manifest in various ways, often affecting motivation, focus and overall sense of purpose. So, in concrete terms, what would these signs showing a lack of clear goals or direction look like?

Here are some common indicators evidencing lack of clear goals and/or direction:

◊ **Lack of motivation**: without clear goals, it is easy to feel unmotivated or directionless, as there is no specific objective to work toward. You may find yourself procrastinating or feeling uninterested in tasks.

- ◊ **Feeling stuck or Lost:** You might feel like you are going through the motions without making meaningful progress, leading to a sense of being *"stuck"* in your personal or professional life.

- ◊ **Frequent indecision**: Without clear goals decision-making becomes difficult because there is no clear framework for choosing the best course of action. This can lead to overthinking and hesitation in making even small choices.

- ◊ **Lack of Focus:** When goals are unclear, it is easy to become distracted by irrelevant tasks or activities that don't align with any specific purpose. This can lead to scattered attention and decreased productivity.

- ◊ **Feeling Overwhelmed**: The absence of goals can cause you to feel a sense of overwhelm. This is because you may feel as if there is so much to do but don't know where to begin or what to prioritise.

- ◊ **Procrastination:** This topic comes up often as you explore this self-empowerment journey, and you will see repeatedly, that without clear targets to aim for, it is easy to delay taking action. This is often due to a lack of clarity on what needs to be done or how to start.

- ◊ **Unfulfilled or Disconnected**: You might experience a general sense of dissatisfaction or lack of fulfilment, feeling disconnected from your purpose or unsure of what you want to achieve in life.

- ◊ Then there is the feeling of **Low confidence**. This shows up as the inability to track your progress or celebrate small wins, which can erode your confidence, and make you feel as if you are not moving forward or accomplishing anything significant.

Overall, the signs listed above suggest that without a clear sense of direction or defined goals, it becomes difficult to make progress, and this leads to feelings of frustration or stagnation. The important thing to note is, there are solutions to these problems, and these are outlined below, as steps that can get to the heart of these problems by putting you in control of your life.

LACK OF CLEAR GOALS/DIRECTION - *SOLUTIONS*

To address the issue of lacking clear goals or direction, it is essential to take deliberate steps that will help to clarify your objectives, give you a sense of purpose and enhance your motivation. There are also practical steps to get you started. This involves spending time to reflect on your values, interests and what really matters to you. Create specific, measurable, achievable, relevant and time-bound (SMART) goals.

Let's break these down for greater understanding of how to tackle them below.

⇒ **Self-Reflection**

Self-Reflection is a key element in assessing your values and your passions. Spend time reflecting on what matters to you most. What do you really enjoy? What are your core values? This reflection will give you a sense of purpose and guide you to set goals that aligned with your interests. In addition, you should identify your strengths and weaknesses. Understand what your skills and areas for improvement are, and this will help you to create realistic and achievable goals.

⇒ **Define Your Vision**

What is your plan? Every builder first has a vision, then a plan of what his building will look like, and what tools he will need to complete his project. You, like the builder also need a plan. You can start by **creating a vision statement**. In a practical way, this can be outlining what you want to achieve in different areas of your life – career, relationships, personal growth, health, etc. Having a clear vision will give you a sense of direction and increase your motivation to complete your plan. You will also need to think of the long-term. **Make this plan achievable** as you picture where you want to be in 1, 3, or 5-years' time. This helps you to break down broad goals into more manageable short-term objectives.

⇒ **Set Specific, Measurable Goals**

Once your vision is clear, you need to have a plan for achieving, and a method for accessing how you are going to progress. You can do this by using **SMART goals.** S.M.A.R.T is an acronym (**S**pecific, **M**easurable, **A**chievable, **R**elevant and **T**ime-bound), which is used as a system to establish criteria for effective goal setting and developing objectives. This SMART goal system is commonly used in business marketing strategies, project management and overall growth, because it encourages you to investigate your market and evaluate how your business is stacking up. Its effectiveness shows that it is a good way to plan the steps needed to meet the long-term goals to achieve your aims.

Similarly, in this self-empowerment journey to discover the power within you, your self-discovery is like your project plan, which must have criteria to measure success. Therefore, you will need to set the goals that are **Specific, Measurable, Achievable, Relevant, and Time-bound** to your self-empowerment journey. Highlighting the steps you will need to take, as well as the criteria for achieving your set goals, is a good strategy, because the framework helps to turn vague ideas into concrete, actionable plans. One approach is to start small, by breaking down large, overwhelming goals into smaller, actionable steps. This makes your goals feel more achievable and allows you to build momentum as you make progress.

⇒ **Prioritise Your goals**

To prioritise your goals, you should focus on what matters most. With a clear vision in mind, identify the goals that are most important to you, and focus your energy on them. Trying to achieve everything at once can lead to burnout and confusion. At the same time, you should learn to say *"NO."* Without clear goals, it is easy to become distracted by irrelevant opportunities or tasks. Learn to say *"NO"* to things that don't align with your priorities. Most of us struggle with setting boundaries because we are afraid of seeming rude, afraid of disappointing people, afraid of losing relationships and afraid of not being liked. But here's the reframe that changed things for me: Boundaries aren't about pushing people away - they are about making room for healthy connection. The fact is, you can't pour from an empty cup, and you can't show up as your best self, when you feel resentful, overwhelmed by agreeing to put others first.

⇒ **Create an Action Plan**

Develop a step-by-step plan. Once you have specific goals, break them down into tasks and deadlines. When you have a clear plan, it allows you to stay organised and track your progress. Moreover, you should set milestones to celebrate small wins along the way, to help keep your motivation high, and to reinforce the sense of accomplishment.

⇒ **Track your Progress**

You should evaluate your goals regularly. Assessing your progress regularly helps you to see if you are on track, or if any adjustments need to be made. Tracking also helps you to stay focused and aware of where you stand. Another important point to consider is to be flexible. Sometimes, life circumstances change, and you may need to adjust your goals or timelines. Being flexible ensures that you stay aligned with your overall vision.

⇒ **Seek Guidance or Mentorship**

Sometimes, discussing your thoughts with a mentor, coach or friend can help you gain clarity and perspective on your goals. They can provide advice, support and encouragement. If you prefer to make guidance more official, you can consider getting professional help. In fact, if you are struggling to define your direction, a Career Coach or Counsellor can guide you to uncover your purpose and help you with your actionable goals.

⇒ **Build Accountability**

Having someone to check in with regularly can help keep you accountable. Whether it is a friend, colleague or mentor, sharing your goals ensures that you remain committed. On my own weight loss journey, I found it more motivating when I had to report to my son about my weekly performance and monthly gains. I discovered that my level of determination increased, my pride in achieving those small gains, felt more meaningful, especially as I was getting feedback from, not only my son, but I considered it partly official; the fact that he is a qualified Professional Fitness Instructor. For example, for my overall health and wellness plan, my **Vision Board** tracked the following data below:

I typed up my vision and expectations for changes to my **Health & Wellness, Nutrition, Exercise and**

Sleep. My rationale for this tracked information made me look at the plan in great depth and with seriousness. Recorded data such as ***Why Change/What it Means/ and How Will I Change;*** with ***my name and a starting date,*** made the projected plan more realistic with concrete information, and measurable outcomes. This also generated a certain amount of excitement, knowing that I would be reporting to someone, made me more determined to expect success in my weight loss journey.

Furthermore, to build more accountability, you can use tools such as productivity **apps or journalling**, to track daily tasks and progress. I certainly created my own journalling, not only to track results but also to create weekly diet schedules, record baseline data on how my body was changing and **the soft outcomes** I had gained. Soft outcomes included information such as the quality of my sleep, the impact on my overall mood, changes to my hair, skin and other noticeable improvements that gave me an overall picture of how I was benefitting from my weight loss journey.

⇒ **Practice Patience and Self-compassion**

Make no mistake, the process of change is not always instant. Finding clear goals and direction is a process that takes time and self-reflection. You should allow time for growth, by being patient with yourself, as you explore and refine your objectives. It is important to avoid being overly critical, if you don't have everything figured out immediately. Give yourself the grace to grow and adjust along the way. At the same time, you should **stay open to new opportunities**. Sometimes, new opportunities or experiences may arise that shift your goals. So, stay open to change and be willing to re-evaluate and adjust your direction as needed.

Here are some **Affirmations** together with an **Inner Shift Journal Practice**, and a daily **Embodiment Action**, to help you deal with lack of clear goals or direction, as you delve deeper into your transformational journey.

Affirmations for lack of clear goals or direction:

1. "Clarity comes as I act."
2. "I trust the process of discovery."
3. "I create space for inspiration."
4. "I move forward, even in uncertainty."
5. "My purpose is unfolding."

Journal Prompts:

1. What brings me joy or energy, even in small doses?
2. Where do I feel pulled, even if I don't understand why?
3. If I didn't need a "perfect" goal, what would I pursue today?

Embodiment Action:
Try something new or revisit a forgotten interest. Write about the experience.

By following these steps, you can move from feeling directionless to having a clear set of goals that guide your actions, develop your motivation, and ultimately empower you to take meaningful steps toward your desired future.

By now, you will begin to see the interconnectedness between these roadblocks and the need to identify them within your life, because we often ignore them to our peril. The relationship between the lack of having clear goals or direction, and the next roadblock being discussed, which is toxic relationships, is obvious. This is because the lack of clear goals often creates a sense of confusion and disempowerment, which can make you more vulnerable to entering or staying in toxic relationships.

When you lack a sense of purpose or direction in your own life, you may rely on external sources, such as relationships, for validation or a sense of identity. In such cases, being in a toxic relationship can take advantage of this uncertainty, by manipulating your emotions, undermining your self-worth, and preventing your personal growth. Without clear goals, you may struggle to set boundaries or recognise unhealthy dynamics. This lack of clarity, combined with the negative influence of a toxic relationship, can keep you feeling stuck and powerless. This makes it even more difficult for you to reclaim control over your life.

TOXIC RELATIONSHIPS – *ROADBLOCK*

Let's talk about toxic relationships. Many people are in relationships where they feel drained, unsupported or constantly have to deal with conflict. If this is your situation, then begin to evaluate your relationships and consider if certain people are holding you back, draining your energy, or making you feel unworthy.

So, how do you define what a toxic relationship is? Toxic relationships are characterised by harmful patterns of behaviour that undermine your well-being, your self-esteem and your emotional health. These relationships are marked by manipulation, control, constant criticism, and an imbalance of power: where your needs and emotions are consistently prioritised over your partner's. Whether it is a romantic partnership, a friendship, or even family dynamics, toxic relationships can gradually erode your sense of self-worth, leaving you feeling drained, confused and powerless.

Recognising the signs of a toxic relationship is crucial, because staying in such a relationship can hinder your personal growth and lead to emotional distress, and prevent you from living a fulfilling, empowered life. A toxic relationship may start off well, subtle at first, and even begin trouble-free, but over time, it might become more evident and harmful to your emotional well-being.

Broken down further, here are some common indicators of a toxic relationship.

- ◊ **Constant Criticism:** One person frequently belittles or criticizes the other, often masking it as "constructive feedback." This can erode your self-esteem and create feelings of inadequacy.

- ◊ **Lack of Trust:** Trust is fundamental to healthy relationships, but in a toxic relationship, there is often suspicion, dishonesty, or betrayal, making it difficult to feel secure.

- ◊ **Manipulation and control:** One partner may try to manipulate or control the other, using guilt, threats, or emotional blackmail to get their way. This can lead to a loss of your autonomy and independence.

- ◊ **Emotional or Physical Abuse:** Any form of abuse – whether verbal, emotional, physical or sexual – is a clear sign of toxicity. Abuse can be overt or subtle, but it always leaves you feeling degraded and fearful.

- ◊ **Chronic Unhappiness:** If the relationship consistently leaves you feeling drained, anxious or unhappy, this is a sign that the dynamic is toxic and not supportive of your emotional needs.

◊ **Lack of support:** In toxic relationships, one person may dismiss the other's needs, dreams, or aspirations. Instead of offering support, they may belittle or ignore your goals and desires.

◊ **Feeling Drained or Devalued:** Toxic relationships often make you feel exhausted, devalued or emotionally empty. Instead of feeling uplifted or validated, you might feel continuously worn out or unimportant.

◊ **Frequent Drama or conflict:** Constant arguments, miscommunications, or unnecessary drama, can indicate you are in a toxic dynamic. Healthy relationships tend to involve conflict resolution, but in toxic ones, conflicts are never resolved; in fact, they may even escalate.

◊ **Isolation:** A toxic partner might attempt to isolate you from your friends, family or other support networks. This is so they could exert more control over you. They may constantly criticise your relationships with others or make you feel guilty for spending time apart from them, to make you obey them and result in your self-imposed isolation.

◊ **Feeling Obligated, Not Appreciated:** In toxic relationships, you might feel like you "have to" stay or perform a certain way, rather than feeling loved and appreciated for who you are. This obligation can make you feel trapped and undervalued.

Overall, this roadblock to your empowerment is very debilitating, because it robs you of a sense of self-esteem in your life. However, recognising these signs is the first step toward protecting yourself and reclaiming your well-being. If you notice these patterns, it may be necessary to reassess your relationship and seek support or guidance to help you make healthier decisions.

TOXIC RELATIONSHIPS – *SOLUTIONS*

It would be very easy to just tell you to set healthy boundaries, limit contact with toxic individuals, and prioritise relationships that encourage your growth and positivity. But how would doing this work in practice? Dealing with toxic relationships requires a combination of self-awareness, boundary-setting, and, in some cases, making the difficult decision to end the relationship.

Potentially, you can tackle your toxic relationship problems as follows:

⇒ **Accept you have the problem**

The first step is to acknowledge that your relationship is toxic. This involves recognising the signs and being honest with yourself about the patterns of behaviour that are harmful to you, such as manipulation, abuse or lack of respect. In identifying the impact of this in your life, you need to understand how the relationship is affecting your emotional, mental and physical well-being. Therefore, recognising the negative impact on your life overall, will help to reinforce your need for change.

⇒ **Set Clear Boundaries**

You will need to set clear boundaries, by defining your personal limits and communicating them to your partner. Boundaries help to protect your emotional space and assert your own needs. Whilst this be tricky as the start, stick to your boundaries. Be consistent about enforcing these boundaries, even if the other person tries to push back against them. The fact is respect for your boundaries is essential for a healthy relationship.

⇒ **Seek Professional Support**

If you need to seek professional help, such as therapy or counsel, you can choose to either get support on your own or as a couple. Working with a professional can help you better understand the dynamics of your relationship, with whom you can also learn how to develop strategies for coping or improving communication. In fact, sometimes joining a support group of people who have experienced similar toxic relationships can provide emotional support and valuable insights.

⇒ **Self-Care and Personal Growth focus**

Looking after yourself and prioritising your wellbeing cannot be emphasised enough. You need to take time for activities that nurture your physical and mental health, such as exercise, hobbies and spending time with supportive people. More importantly, rediscover your old interests because in toxic relationships, you tend to lose sight of your personal passions and goals, whilst you prioritise others. Therefore, you need to reconnect with things that bring you joy and fulfilment, to regain your sense of individuality.

⇒ **Open communication**

If possible, you need to have honest conversations, where you can discuss your concerns with the other person in a calm and respectful manner. You need to express how their behaviour is affecting you and see if they are willing to change. At the same time, you will need to listen and understand their line of reasoning, as this amounts to effective communication. Effective communication is key in this scenario as it ensures that you express your feelings clearly, and that you also listen to the other person's perspective.

⇒ **Limit/Cut Ties if Necessary**

In facing the reality of your situation, you may, where relevant, gradually need to distance yourself. In some cases, it may be necessary to do so emotionally or physically from the toxic person. This could mean reducing the time spent together, to taking breaks. Additionally, should this become necessary, you may need to end the relationship altogether. If the toxicity continues despite efforts to address it, ending the relationship may be the healthiest option. Opting to end the relationship can be especially important, if there is abuse or persistent harm involved.

⇒ Building a Support Network

Given the nature of this roadblock, a good advice would be to surround yourself with positive people. Having a strong support network of friends, family and mentors can offer encouragement and help to reinforce your self-worth. It is also a kind of seeking validation from healthy sources, where you rely on people who support and uplift, rather than those who drain, abuse or manipulate you.

⇒ Empower Yourself

As you develop a sense of self-work and your self-esteem grows, remind yourself of your value and that you deserve healthy, respectful relationships. Building self-esteem can make it easier to take the necessary steps to remove yourself from toxic situations. See it as a form of strengthening or a way of developing your emotional resilience, because this helps you to cope with challenges and pressures from toxic relationships, without letting them define your sense of self.

⇒ Educate Yourself About Healthy Relationships

Another way to build your resolve, is to learn about what makes healthy dynamics. In other words, educate yourself about what constitutes a healthy relationship, including mutual respect, trust, communication and emotional support. This knowledge helps you recognise when a relationship is unhealthy. By understanding the patterns of toxicity, you are familiarising yourself with common toxic behaviours such as manipulation, gaslighting, or control. Ultimately, this will help you to avoid falling into similar patterns in the future.

⇒ **Patience is a Virtue**

You will need to give yourself time as you heal from a toxic relationship. Be patient with yourself, and refrain from rushing into another relationship too soon. Give yourself space and time to process your emotions and experiences, before making decisions about moving forward.

Here are some **Affirmations** together with an **Inner Shift Journal Practice**, and a daily **Embodiment Action**, to help you deal with toxic relationships as you delve deeper into your transformational journey.

Affirmations for toxic relationships:

1. *"I deserve love that uplifts and respects me."*
2. *"I release what no longer aligns with my well-being."*
3. *"My boundaries are sacred and necessary."*
4. *"I am worthy of relationships that nourish me."*
5. *"I choose peace over chaos."*

Journal Prompts:

1. Are there relationships in my life that leave me feeling drained or small?
2. What are my current boundaries and where might they need strengthening?
3. What would it look like to honour my worth in all my relationships?

Embodiment Action:
Set (or reinforce) one boundary today - even if it's just with yourself. Reflect on how it feels.

Ultimately, the solutions to toxic relationships involve taking responsibility for your well-being, setting boundaries and deciding whether the relationship can be improved or if it is best to move on. It is important to remember that you deserve respect, kindness and support in all relationships, so prioritise getting them.

You should now be feeling relieved with the information so far, since it helps to bring clarity to your life, illuminating areas of your life that you either took for granted or ignored; believing they did not require any change. However, just as we have with toxic relationships, the next roadblock to self-empowerment that we will go on to explore, is a habit of demanding perfectionism in your life.

The fact is, toxic relationships and the development of perfectionism often intersect, creating a powerful roadblock to self-empowerment. A slight difference is that in a toxic relationship, especially one that is marked by constant criticism or unrealistic expectations, affects your life negatively, as it may help to develop an obsession for perfectionism. This can come about because within the toxic relationship, you may internalise the negative messages about yourself, that help to develop perfectionistic tendencies about your abilities.

For example, the need to persistently meet impossible standards can stem from the fear of judgement or rejection within the toxic relationship, leading to a constant pursuit of perfection to gain approval or avoid conflict. This cycle of striving for unattainable goals often leaves you feeling inadequate, stressed, and defeated, because you feel you can never meet the overly high expectations placed on you. In turn, perfectionism further diminishes your self-worth and stifles your personal growth. The result is that perfectionism makes it difficult for you to embrace your authentic self and achieve your true empowerment. So, what is Perfectionism in practice, and how does this manifest as a roadblock to your self-empowerment? Let's explore this in the next chapter.

PERFECTIONISM – *ROADBLOCK*

And what about an obsession with being perfect as the rule, rather than an exception? In a nutshell, perfectionism is to do with those who obsess over details, have a fear of making mistakes, or do not finish tasks because they feel they are not *'perfect'*. This may have its deep root in many sources, but you need to identify this trait. If you often feel that nothing is ever good enough or that you cannot move forward unless or until everything is flawless, perfectionism might be a roadblock to your self-empowerment.

Perfectionism is identified as excessively striving for flawlessness or perfection. In addition, it is accompanied by an intense fear of making mistakes, which is a significant roadblock to self-empowerment. On one hand, setting high standards can sometimes drive success, but on the other hand, perfectionism often leads to unrealistic expectations and a constant sense of failure, when achievements are made.

Individuals who struggle with perfectionism tend to focus on their shortcomings and are overly critical of themselves. This can erode your self-esteem and create feelings of inadequacy. Such a mindset prevents you from seeing mistakes as opportunities to grow and consequently limit your ability to take risks or explore new opportunities. In fact, instead of developing self-confidence, and personal growth, perfectionism keeps you trapped in a cycle of self-doubt and fear. Ultimately, it hinders your ability to fully embrace your full potential and empower yourself. But what are the signs of perfectionism, and how do you recognise it in your life? Perfectionism can manifest in many ways, affecting both your thoughts and behaviour, so here are some common signs:

◊ **Constant self-Criticism**

There is nothing wrong about being critical about something that you've done but when you constantly criticise yourself for not being good enough, even if your performance is objectively excellent, it is a sign of perfectionism. In fact, you may even focus more on your mistakes or flaws than on your successes.

◊ **Fear of Making Mistakes**

Again, in trying to do well in anything the thought of making a mistake is something that may cross your mind, whether you are an athlete, a performer, or speaker. However, it is the intense fear of failure or making mistakes, leading to avoidance of challenges or taking extreme precautions to avoid errors, that categorise perfectionism. This fear may paralyse you from taking risks or trying out new things.

◊ **Setting Unrealistically High Standards**

When you set standards that are often impossible to meet, or when you push yourself to perform at an unattainable level, this might point to perfectionism as a roadblock to your self-empowerment. In fact, the feeling is more marked when these standards are not met, and you feel deeply disappointed or inadequate in yourself.

◊ **Procrastination**

We have seen this trait in other roadblocks above before. However, paradoxically, as a perfectionist you may procrastinate because you are afraid of not being able to complete a task perfectly. This can lead to delays, as the pressure to get everything right might cause you to avoid doing it altogether.

◊ **Difficulty Delegating**

As a perfectionist, you may find it hard to trust others with tasks because you think no one else can meet your standards. This often results in micro-managing or doing everything yourself. This can lead to over-pressuring yourself and burnout. Additionally, if you are struggling with feedback, it's important to know that most perfectionists are overly defensive or discouraged when they receive constructive feedback on something they have done. It is because they see it as a sign of failure, rather than an opportunity to improve.

◊ **Constant Comparison to Others**

If you frequently compare yourself to others and feel that you fall short, even if you are doing well in comparison, you may be developing perfectionist tendencies. This can lead to feelings of jealousy or inadequacy. Overall, this creates a negative impact on relationships. Perfectionism can strain your relationship because you may have unrealistic expectations of others around you or those in your life, or you may be overly critical of their actions. This leads to frustration or conflict and tension in your relationship.

◊ **Difficulty Enjoying Achievements**

The problem with being a perfectionist is that you become so hard on yourself that even after completing a task successfully, you might not allow yourself to feel satisfied or proud. Instead, you focus on what could have been done better or what went wrong - there is a sense that it's either all or nothing. Perfectionists often view situations in black-and-white terms; meaning, either everything is perfect, or it is a failure. This thinking prevents you from recognising the value in progress or in partial success.

Overall, these signs reflect how perfectionism can negatively affect mental well-being, productivity, and relationships. They can also prevent individuals from embracing mistakes, finding balance and feeling empowered. However, because this book is about self-empowerment and finding the hidden power within, we are effectively, in this first section of the book, highlighting the problems that hinder self-empowerment, and providing solutions to them, in order to activate the power within you. So, what can be done about perfectionism? Firstly, you will need to shift your focus to progress, rather than perfection, and allow yourself to make mistakes and learn from them, without judgement.

PERFECTIONISM – *SOLUTIONS*

Overcoming perfectionism involves shifting your mindset, setting realistic expectations and developing self-compassion. Let's look at some effective solutions to help you break free from the cycle of perfectionism.

⇒ **Set Realistic and Flexible Goals**

Firstly, you need to set goals that are challenging but achievable. Instead of striving for perfection, aim for "good quality" and recognise that mistakes are a natural part of growth. In other words, you need to adjust your expectations. Additionally, you should break down larger tasks into smaller, more manageable steps. This allows you to focus on progress, rather than perfection and prevents you from feeling overwhelmed.

⇒ **Practice Self-compassion**

As with the toxic relationship, and focusing on yourself in that relationship, you should practice self-compassion by treating yourself with the same kindness and understanding that you would offer a friend. You should also accept that it is okay to make mistakes and that no one is perfect. Be aware of negative self-talk, so that when you catch yourself being overly critical, you can replace those thoughts with more balanced, supportive ones. Overall, you should focus on the effort you put in, rather than only on the outcome.

⇒ Embrace Imperfection

Adjusting your mindset here is important. You need to see mistakes as opportunities to learn. Understanding that mistakes are an essential part of learning and personal growth is important in strengthening your sense of self. Rather than view mistakes as failures, see them as chances to improve and try again. An essential element here is letting go of being perfect in small things. Start with smaller, low stakes tasks and intentionally allow yourself to leave imperfections. This can help desensitise you to the fear of making mistakes and help you feel comfortable with imperfection.

Instead of thinking in extremes, you should reframe situations by practicing seeing the grey areas and accepting that progress and effort are valuable. For example, you must get rid of the *"I must do this perfectly or it's a failure."* For, *"Okay it wasn't quite what I expected but I can now see how to improve it next time."* As simple as it sounds, it can be difficult to accept by others.

⇒ Learn to Delegate

Letting go or trusting others is essential to adjusting your mindset where perfectionism is concerned. Delegate tasks when possible and trust that others can perform tasks without needing to meet your standards.

This will help you to reduce the pressure you place on yourself. Moreover, you must learn to accept different approaches. In other words, understand that there are often many ways to do things, and perfection is not the only option. Allow others to approach tasks in their own way, you may be surprised!

⇒ **Focus on the Process, not just the Outcome**

This is great advice as it opens your understanding to your journey, which is to enjoy it! Shift your focus from looking solely at the result; instead, appreciate the process and the effort you are putting in. This can help reduce the pressure to achieve perfection and allow you to find satisfaction in the experience. Overall, it enables you to recognise that progress, no matter how small, is an important step toward achieving long-term goals.

⇒ **Set Boundaries and Take Breaks**

As a perfectionist, you may tend to have a persistent need to drive yourself, or to be hard on yourself, physically, mentally and emotionally. Avoid over-committing by learning to say *NO and* set boundaries to prevent yourself from taking on too much. This helps reduce stress and keeps you from spreading yourself too thin, in your quest for perfection. In fact, you should schedule rest or breaks. Give yourself permission to take breaks to recharge. Downtime is crucial for mental health, and it also helps prevent burnout.

⇒ Seek Support

You should not feel too proud to seek help. Consider therapy by talking to a therapist, especially one providing cognitive-behavioural therapy (CBT), who can help you identify and address perfectionistic thinking patterns. A therapist can guide you in challenging unhelpful beliefs and develop healthier coping strategies. As already suggested for obsessive habits, connect with supportive people. Surround yourself with people who encourage you to embrace imperfection, and who offer unconditional support, rather than reinforce high, unrealistic standards.

⇒ Celebrate Small Wins

It is important to acknowledge your achievements by taking time to celebrate your successes, no matter how small. Recognising and appreciating what you've accomplished helps shift the focus from what is lacking, to what has been achieved. This is a belief I have held tenaciously on to, as a School Headteacher of over 30 years; using celebratory occasions with students (at the *end of each week, end of each term*, and end of *each academic year*), as a motivating factor to succeed. This was done to reinforce and celebrate in a concrete way, the essence of our motto, which was, "*I am Somebody Great.*" It was also a time when the students enjoyed and felt proud for the opportunity to showcase their achievements to their peers and teachers and guests, *(e.g. parents, visitors, and invited officials from local government)*, to witness and celebrated what they had achieved.

The most noticeable benefit of these occasions was that after each event, the students increased the quality of their engagement with their education by at least 50%, year on year. This included students of all abilities, e.g. those with Special Education Needs (SEN). As we recorded the students' *"hard"* outcomes, which was tracked by baseline data, it enabled us to track their results of performance in school, but also, I made it my duty to also track other benefits, such as the *"soft"* outcomes, gained by the students.

Soft outcomes included their attitude to learning, the extra effort they made, e.g. how they felt about their teachers and peers, the way they treated others around them and their attitude and mannerisms to their whole notion of what "school" really means to them. It was a win-win situation, and one that I still endorse, (over 3 decades now), with enthusiasm and passion. This was possible because I recognised, right at the start, that the small *weekly* wins, motivated the need to gain *termly* wins and accumulatively, it helped to maintain the need to also sustain success over the *academic year,* for the grand finale, in our *"Annual Celebration of Achievement"* events, to mark the end of the school year. This provided concrete evidence that celebrating small wins, does work!

⇒ **Mindfulness and Stress-Relief Techniques**

Mindfulness techniques such as meditation or deep breathing can help you stay present and also reduce the anxiety that often accompanies perfectionism. If you engage in regular relaxation practices, such as yoga or walks in nature, this can help reduce the stress and pressure that is associated with perfectionistic tendencies. I believe that by implementing these solutions, you can gradually break free from the grip of perfectionism, and embrace a more balanced, self-compassionate and empowered approach to life.

Here are some **Affirmations** together with an **Inner Shift Journal Practice**, and a daily **Embodiment Action**, to help you deal with Perfectionism, as you delve deeper into your transformational journey.

Affirmations for perfectionism:

1. "Done is better than perfect."
2. "I embrace progress over perfection."
3. "Imperfection is a sign of authenticity."
4. "I am allowed to be a work in progress."
5. "I let go of unrealistic expectations."

Journal Prompts:

1. Where in my life am I holding back because something isn't perfect yet?
2. What am I afraid will happen if I make a mistake or show flaws?
3. How might embracing imperfection free me?

Embodiment Action:
Share or finish something "imperfect" - a draft, post, email, or idea - and reflect on the outcome.

In summary, perfectionism fuels the fear of failure, and makes you avoid risks, procrastinate, or never feel *"good enough,"* about yourself. Ultimately it prevents you from stepping into your full potential. Similarly, limiting beliefs - such as *"I'm not smart enough"* or *"I don't deserve success"* - reinforce feelings of inadequacy and self-doubt, keeping you trapped in a cycle of hesitation and inaction.

Both perfectionism and the next disempowering roadblock that we will look at - *limiting beliefs* - stem from deep-seated fears and negative self-perceptions. This makes empowerment difficult, by restricting the mindset and behaviours that are necessary for your progress. Overcoming these roadblocks require a shift in perspective - embracing growth over flawlessness, and challenging self-imposed limitations to step into your true power.

LIMITING BELIEFS – *ROADBLOCK*

How many times have you heard the expression, *"I'm not good enough!"* You may even have said it yourself, *"I can't do this"* or *"This isn't for people like me."* These expressions are manifestations of strong roadblocks, since stating them means you are reinforcing negativity deep within your subconscious. Be aware that such beliefs consistently hold you back from pursuing opportunities, from trying new things, and from believing in your potential. In fact, they are contrary to you unlocking the power within you.

Limiting beliefs are often shown in crafty but powerful ways, shaping your thoughts, your behaviours, and decisions. From the list below, you will see there are many different types of limiting beliefs which can invade your life in subtle ways. Therefore, it's important to identify them to consciously take steps to eliminate them from your life because of the stifling effect they have on your power. Here is a list of some common signs of limiting beliefs which act as roadblocks to your empowerment:

1. **Negative Self-Talk** – Frequently saying things like, *"I can't," "I'm not good enough,"* or *"I'll never succeed."*
2. **Fear of Failure** – Avoiding challenges or new opportunities due to fear of making mistakes.

3. **Procrastination** – Delaying action because of doubt in one's ability to succeed.
4. **Seeking External Validation** – Relying on others' approval to feel worthy or capable.
5. **All-or-Nothing Thinking** – Believing success must be perfect or it doesn't count.
6. **Feeling Stuck** – Having a strong desire for change but believing it's impossible or out of reach.
7. **Excuses and Justifications** – Saying things like, *"It's too late for me,"* or *"People like me don't succeed."*
8. **Comparing Yourself to Others** – Believing others are naturally more capable or deserving.
9. **Low Self-Worth** – Feeling undeserving of success, happiness, or love.
10. **Resisting Change** – Avoiding growth because it feels too risky or uncomfortable.

LIMITING BELIEFS – *SOLUTIONS*

As you can see, this list is long, and you will probably resonate with some of them. However, recognising these signs is the first step to overcoming limiting beliefs and reclaiming your personal power. Let's look at the solutions for each sign of limiting beliefs, to learn what you can do about them.

⇒ **Negative Self-talk**

If you find yourself involved in negative self-talk, you should reframe this habit with positive affirmations. The fact is, negative self-talk often stems from deeply ingrained beliefs formed through past experiences or societal conditioning. To counteract this, you must become aware of the negative statements you tell yourself and consciously reframe them into positive, empowering affirmations. For example, if you often think, *"I'm not good enough,"* you can challenge this belief by listing your past achievements, no matter how small. The next step is to replace it with a statement like, *"I am capable and constantly growing."* Writing these affirmations down or repeating them daily can help to rewire your brain; by helping it adopt a more constructive and positive inner dialogue.

⇒ **Fear of Failure**

The antidote of being afraid to fail, is that you should adopt a growth mind. This is because the fear of failure can be paralysing. However, it often results from seeing failure as a dead-end, rather than a stepping stone. A growth mindset, as coined by psychologist Carol Dweck, encourages you to view challenges as opportunities to learn rather than as threats to your self-worth. Instead of fearing failure, ask yourself, *"What can I learn from this experience?"* Many successful people - such as Thomas Edison or Oprah Winfrey - experienced failure before achieving greatness. By reframing failure as feedback rather than a reflection of ability, allows you to take more risks and grow with each experience.

⇒ **Procrastination**

Procrastination is often a symptom of overwhelm, and one way to deal with this is to break tasks down into small steps, especially where a task feels too big or difficult to start. Instead of looking at the entire project, you should break it down into the smallest possible step you can take. For example, if you're avoiding writing a report, start by just opening a document and jotting down ideas for five minutes. This small action reduces resistance and builds momentum. Using strategies like the *Pomodoro Technique* - where you work in short, timed intervals then take a break - can also make daunting tasks feel more manageable.

When you do this, even in tiny increments, it's key to overcoming the inertia of procrastination.

⇒ **Seeking External Validation**

Relying on others for approval can make you feel unworthy, unless someone else acknowledges your worth. To break this cycle, start by tuning into your own values and instincts. When making decisions, instead of immediately seeking approval, ask yourself, *"What do I truly want?"* Keep a journal of your achievements and the positive feedback you receive from others to remind yourself of your strengths. Over time, as you celebrate small personal victories and trust your own judgment, you'll rely less on external validation and more on your own sense of self-worth.

⇒ **All-or-Nothing Thinking**

In order to deal with the all-or-nothing modes of thinking, a simplified solution is to embrace progress as you go along, rather than seek perfection. The fact is, perfectionism creates unrealistic standards that make it hard to start or complete tasks. If you believe that something must be flawless to be worthwhile, you may never act. Instead, you should shift your focus to *progress* rather than perfection. Remind yourself that improvement happens in small steps, and that imperfect action is still valuable. Set realistic, flexible goals and acknowledge every step forward as a success. By embracing the mindset that *done is better than perfect,* you are freeing yourself from unnecessary stress and at the same time, it allows room for creativity and learning.

⇒ Feeling Stuck

Feeling stuck often arises from deeply held assumptions about what is or isn't possible. These assumptions may come from past failures, societal expectations, or fear of uncertainty. To challenge these beliefs, ask yourself, *"What evidence do I have that this is true?"* Often, you'll realize that the limitations you've placed on yourself are not as solid as they seem. Surrounding yourself with people who challenge their own limitations, reading stories of resilience, or seeking mentorship can help shift your perspective, and show you that *movement* is always possible.

⇒ Excuses and Justifications

It's easy to blame external circumstances for why things haven't worked out, but this mindset can keep you trapped in inaction. Instead, take ownership of your choices and recognize that while you may not control every situation, you *do* control how you respond. Shift your thinking from, *"I can't because..."* to *"How can I...?"* This small change reframes challenges as problems to be solved, rather than barriers. Personal accountability empowers you to take charge of your life and find creative solutions instead of staying stuck in a cycle of excuses.

⇒ **Comparing Yourself to Others**

Comparison is a common trap that can lead to self-doubt and feelings of inadequacy. Instead of measuring your worth against others, redirect your focus to your own journey and unique strengths. Keep a gratitude journal where you write down things you appreciate about yourself daily. Recognise that everyone has struggles and that social media often presents a filtered version of reality. When you shift from competition to self-appreciation, you'll start seeing your unique qualities and contributions as valuable.

⇒ **Low Self-Worth**

A lack of self-worth often comes from harsh self-judgment and unrealistic expectations. To counter this, practice self-compassion by treating yourself as you would treat a close friend. Instead of criticising yourself for mistakes, remind yourself that everyone has setbacks. Engage in activities that make you feel strong, accomplished, or joyful - whether it's learning a new skill, exercising, or spending time with loved ones. Remember that over time, consistent self-care and self-affirmation will help to reinforce your sense of worthiness.

⇒ **Resisting Change**

Fear of change is natural, but staying in your comfort zone can prevent your growth. To ease into change, start by taking small, calculated risks. For example, if you want to switch careers but feel uncertain, begin by networking with professionals in your desired field or taking a related online course. The more you expose yourself to new experiences, the more adaptable and confident you'll become. Remind yourself that discomfort is often a sign of growth, and every small step outside your comfort zone builds resilience and expands your possibilities.

The following **Affirmations** together with an **Inner Shift Journal Practice**, and a daily **Embodiment Action**, will help you deal with limiting beliefs, as you delve deeper into your transformational journey.

Affirmations for limiting beliefs:

1. *"I am not my past beliefs — I choose new ones today."*
2. *"My potential is limitless and ever-expanding."*
3. *"I question beliefs that hold me back."*
4. *"I rewrite my story with courage and intention."*
5. *"Anything is possible when I believe it is."*

Journal Prompts:

1. *What beliefs about myself or life were passed down to me that I no longer agree with?*
2. *What's a belief I have that keeps me small or stuck?*
3. *What empowering belief could I choose instead?*

Embodiment Action:

Write your new belief on a sticky note or screen background - keep it visible all day.

Each of the above shifts takes time, but with consistent effort, you can break free from limiting beliefs and step into your full potential. Start with manageable steps outside your comfort zone. The more you embrace change, the more confidence you'll build.

OVERWHELM AND BURNOUT – *ROADBLOCK*

In our fast-paced world, where many things demand our 100% attention, there is a tendency to put yourself last, or to accomplish everything at great speed we feel exhausted, stressed or unable to cope with demands. This is a sign of feeling overwhelmed and burnout. Signs of overwhelm and burnout can act as significant roadblocks to empowerment because they drain you mentally, emotionally and physically.

Here are common signs that contribute to being overwhelmed and burnout.

◊ **Overwhelm**

Beginning with overwhelm, this is a prominent sign of mental fatigue. **Mental Fatigue** is shown by having trouble focusing or concentrating, feeling mentally exhausted or having trouble making decisions. Increased feelings of worry or nervousness, especially about tasks or obligations, can cause anxiety. This may be associated with a **lack of motivation.** Feeling unmotivated or uninterested in tasks; even the ones that used to bring you joy or fulfilment, might be a sign of mental fatigue.

Another sign of overwhelm or burnout is **overthinking**. If you are constantly analysing situations or problems, without finding solutions this can lead to a sense of paralysis. In fact, associated with this state is another roadblock – **irritability**. If you experience **short outbursts of temper** or feel emotional with minor stressors, it is a sign of overwhelm or burnout. Additionally, the fall-out from this emotional state can lead to **physical symptoms**. As far as physical symptoms go, feeling tense, with headaches or even gastrointestinal problems, can arise from constant stress and feeling overwhelmed. Of utmost importance is knowing what we can do about it, and this is discussed below.

◊ **Burnout**

If you are feeling emotionally drained or detached from personal or professional life, it may be a sign of burnout. In addition, if you feel a decrease in productivity, creativity or not feeling effective in work or your daily responsibilities, you may be experiencing burnout. Another sign of burnout is a **reduction in your performance or effectiveness in your daily responsibilities.** If your general performance in your daily activities show that there is a decrease in productivity, creativity or effectiveness at work, it may be a sign that you are at the burnout stage.

◊ **Chronic Fatigue**

Another roadblock which is evident by signs of burnout is **chronic fatigue.** Chronic fatigue is presented as persistent tiredness even after rest, or the feeling that you have little to no energy for your daily chores. Additionally, other signs can be having a general sense of apathy or being disinterested in life.

Looking at Overwhelm and Burnout above, show that they can often lead to feelings of incompetence or low self-worth, which in turn undermines your confidence. In addition, if you are feeling overwhelmed, you may struggle to make decisions. This kind of depleted motivation and energy can make it hard to pursue your goals or take steps towards your growth. Therefore, recognising and addressing these signs early, can help lessen their impact, and restore you to a sense of control, that will help you to regain your power.

OVERWHELM & BURNOUT – *SOLUTIONS*

When you are experiencing overwhelm or burnout, it is crucial to take proactive steps to address and manage the situation. Based on the signs discussed above, here are some practical steps to take into consideration when dealing with burnout and overwhelm.

⇒ The first thing to do is to **acknowledge and accept your feelings**. When you identify and accept that you are overwhelmed or burn out, it is the first step in overcoming the situation, because knowing what to do will either reduce or get rid of the problem or minimise its effects on you. So being kind to yourself and accepting that it's okay to feel this way, doesn't mean you are weak or incapable, it means you are ready to tackle the challenges head on and reclaim your control.

⇒ You should **avoid self-blame by being gentle with yourself.** Overwhelm and burnout happen to many people, especially in high stress environments. Self-blame can make it harder to act toward recovery. Another very important step to take is to **prioritise rest and recovery.** Why not take breaks, and step back from your responsibilities to allow yourself time to rest?

Taking the shortest number of breaks, frequently, will help.

⇒ **Sleep is important to aid recovery**. Ensure you are getting adequate sleep, as rest is essential for mental and physical recovery. You should also engage in forms of relaxation. For example, mindfulness can help, with practices such as deep breathing, and meditation, these can help to manage stress and relax the mind.

⇒ As you consciously take back control, you should also **set boundaries and manage your expectations**. For example, a good self-protective step is to learn to say *no* and make decisions that benefit you. Re-evaluate your commitments and set boundaries to avoid taking on too much. Saying *no* is not a failure; it is a way to protect your well-being. And whilst you are at it, if possible, delegate tasks. Share your workload with others and don't be afraid to ask for help. **Delegating responsibilities** can lighten the load and prevent burnout.

⇒ You should also limit distractions by minimising activities or people around you; especially those who drain your energy - the ones who do not bring value or support to your life. By reassessing and re-organising your priorities, you are letting go of things that don't contribute to your well-being or success. In terms of **time management**, you can use tools like calendars, to-do lists or productivity apps, to stay organised and focused on what needs your attention.

⇒ How about **support systems**? If you feel going it alone is challenging, reach out to friends, family or colleagues for emotional support. Sometimes talking things out can provide a fresh perspective on things. On the other hand, if burnout or overwhelm is severe, you should **consider speaking to a therapist or counsellor** to help you manage stress, rebuild your emotional resilience, and offer you coping strategies that will help you pull through.

⇒ At the same time, you should **cultivate healthy habits** – such as undertaking physical exercise, to help reduce stress and improve mental clarity - even going for a short walk can be beneficial here. Then there is the all-important matter of your nutrition! **Eating a balanced diet** can significantly impact your energy levels and mood. Many people's morning ritual is an absolute reliance on cups of coffee or tea, (mostly coffee), to start their day. For some the absolute necessity of this, is a replacement for breakfast, like a drug-infused habit.

⇒ However, you should avoid relying on caffeine or sugar to fuel your day, because they can help to worsen fatigue. Instead, include things in your life that make you happy or help you to relax; hobbies like reading or spending time in nature. You should also **re-engage in activities** that bring you joy or help to reignite passion and motivation you once had.

⇒ **Reflecting and learning why you felt overwhelmed or burned out** in the first place is a valuable approach to evaluating your limits. Check your actions – was it a result of overwork, lack of boundaries or unrealistic expectations? It's important to understand the root cause, as this can help you to prevent the situation for occurring again in the future.

Here are some **Affirmations** together with an **Inner Shift Journal Practice**, and a daily **Embodiment Action**, to help you deal with overwhelm and burnout, as you delve deeper into your transformational journey.

Affirmations for Overwhelm/Burnout:

1. *"I give myself permission to rest and recharge."*
2. *"I do not have to do everything at once."*
3. *"My well-being is my priority."*
4. *"I set healthy boundaries with time and energy."*
5. *"I am allowed to slow down."*

Journal Prompts:

1. What are my top 3 sources of stress or exhaustion right now?
2. What would my ideal rest day or slow day look like?
3. How can I make space to nurture myself this week?

EMBODIMENT ACTION:
Cancel, delegate, or postpone one non-essential task. Use that time to rest or reflect.

In summary, more solutions to dealing with overwhelm and burnout are to do with **prioritising your self-care**, and **setting boundaries**, so that your own needs are included in your schedule of tasks. Then divide the tasks into manageable chunks and take regular breaks; pacing yourself prevents overload, and factors in more enjoyment in what you are doing. By combining immediate steps with long-term strategies, you will begin to alleviate overwhelm and burnout with you being in the driver's seat! It will also help you to reclaim your mental, emotional and physical well-being, and ultimately empower you to move forward.

LACK OF SUPPORT OR RESOURCES – *ROADBLOCK*

Inequality, which is often caused by wealth disparities and cultural/racial privilege for some sections of society, and lack of support and/or resources, is a reality in our world. If you are struggling to make progress due to a lack of knowledge or have no tools or the means of getting social support, these are obvious roadblocks to your empowerment.

Such roadblocks are in situations where you want to move forward but don't have access to the right resources, the right people or the information to help you do so. When a lack of support or resources becomes a roadblock to empowerment, it can feel like you're stuck in a situation where progress seems almost impossible. However, there are several strategies you can employ to overcome these obstacles, that will enable you to still work towards empowerment.

LACK OF SUPPORT OR RESOURCES – *SOLUTIONS*

⇒ **Seek Alternative Sources of Support**

The first thing to do is to **seek alternative sources of support**. This could be expanding your network, so if your current support system is insufficient, you should seek out new connections. You can do this by attending networking events, joining online communities or connecting with like-minded individuals who share similar goals or values. In addition, you should **consider mentorship and guidance.** This could be finding a mentor or coach who can give you advice, guidance and emotional support. Even if they don't have all the resources you need, their knowledge and experience can be invaluable.

⇒ **Peer Support**

Another consideration is **peer support**. You can seek out peer groups or support circles, where people share similar situations. Sharing experiences can be a huge source of motivation and encouragement. In addition, these groups will become invaluable to you on your list of contacts. The fact is, everything may not be readily available to you, but you certainly can **leverage your existing resources** more effectively. In other words, maximise what you have by making a list of what you have at your disposal, whether it's time, skills, knowledge or access to certain tools. Even limited resources can be used creatively to make progress. In other words, consider how you can **re-purpose what you have** in new ways. This could be using free online tools to learn new skills or finding alternative materials for a project.

⇒ **Resource Sharing**

Another way is to **consider resource-sharing**. If you are part of a group or organisation, look for opportunities to pool resources. Collaborative efforts can often unlock hidden resources that can be of mutual benefit to everyone involved.

⇒ **Self-Education**

Then how about **investing in educating yourself**? When formal resources are lacking, you could focus on self-empowerment through learning. There are many free and low-cost resources, (*e.g. online courses, YouTube videos, webinars, books, podcasts)*, that can help you acquire skills and knowledge needed to progress. Sometimes the lack of resources is more about skill gaps, than material limitations, so you should focus on building your own skills – whether it's learning how to manage finances better, improve productivity, or acquire technical expertise on a subject.

⇒ **Community Resources**

Another solution to personal lack is finding accessible **community resources**. There are many non-profits and local organisations who offer support; whether it's financial assistance, training programs, or access to resources. You could consider volunteering in one of these groups, because it's also a good way to build relationships and networks that offer both emotional and material support.

⇒ **Crowdfunding & Grants**

For those who are lacking financial resources, you could consider applying for available **crowdfunding and grants**. You could start by exploring crowdfunding platforms or looking into grants and fellowships that might align with your goals or needs. Many foundations offer financial support for creative projects, educational endeavours or community-building efforts. The fact is, you must think outside the box when your resources are limited. In such times, **your creativity** can be a powerful tool also. Why not brainstorm unconventional ways to achieve your goals by trading or finding free alternatives to expensive tools or services?

⇒ **Volunteering/Time Exchange**

Alternatively, you could consider **offering your skills or time in exchange** for what you need. Negotiating and coming to mutually beneficial arrangements, without the need for money, can be a great resourceful way of getting what you need. However, it is a fact that depending on what is needed, some solutions can be more challenging to overcome than others; especially where systemic barriers are more entrenched.

⇒ **Advocate for Change**

However, if you are facing systemic barriers to support or resources, (in a workplace, community or organisation, you can **raise awareness** of this or consider taking up the mantle yourself, and **advocate for change**. This could involve speaking to decision-makers, organising petitions or raising awareness about the lack of resources, to create a dialogue around potential solutions. In some cases, you can **lobby for resources** by working with others who share your concerns, to advocate for better resource allocation. Whether through formal channels, community meetings or public campaigns, collective action can bring a more focused attention to the need for more support; and in any case, unless you try, you won't know what could be accessible to you. The fact is, some adverse situations, might actually present opportunities for you to become **self-sufficient**.

We've experienced during the COVID-19 period (2019-2022), when many people globally were forced to adopt self-sufficiency approaches to dealing with the pandemic, and this had a positive effect on their lives as they were able to build mindsets of lasting self-reliance. Learning how to do more with less, developing strong problem-solving skills, and becoming more adaptable in the face of challenges, can sometimes bring out great empowerment skills in us. Even when things feel difficult, progress may take time, but consistent effort leads to growth.

⇒ **Entrepreneurship**

Therefore, you might want to **start something from scratch or identify gaps** or needs in the market or in your community and create your own opportunities. **Entrepreneurship** often thrives in environments where resources are scarce, but creativity and innovation can be abundant!

At the same time, I list below relevant **Affirmations**, together with an **Inner Shift Journal Practice**, and a daily **Embodiment Action**, to help you deal with the Lack of Support/Resources, as you delve deeper into your self-empowerment journey.

Affirmations for lack of support and resources:

1. "I am open to receiving help and support."
2. "The right resources find me at the right time."
3. "I am not alone; I am guided and supported."
4. "I create new paths even when old ones aren't available."
5. "I trust in my resourcefulness and resilience."

Journal Prompts:

1. *Where do I feel unsupported - and have I clearly asked for help?*
2. *What internal or external resources do I already have that I may overlook?*
3. *If support was guaranteed, what would I do differently?*

EMBODIMENT ACTION:
Reach out for help, advice, or guidance - no matter how small - and write about how it felt.

Finally, you should practice expressing gratitude by recognising the resources you do have, no matter how small. Research led by Dr. Roberts Emmons, the world's foremost scientific expert on gratitude, showed that those who engage in daily gratitude practices demonstrate a 23% elevation in baseline serotonin levels, thereby reducing anxiety and enhancing attentional control. Therefore, **shifting your perspective** of the scenario where you consider the *glass being half-full, instead of being half-empty,* can help reduce feelings of abject lack and instead empower you to act with whatever is available.

UNRESOLVED PAST ISSUES – *ROADBLOCK*

Many of us put on a brave face, so that to the external world all is well and we appear to be coping or have no issues. However, in many cases, holding on to past trauma, regret, guilt or anger, presents as another roadblock that impacts our current decisions and behaviour. We identify these traits by reflecting on past experiences that may still affect our present lives. If unresolved issues are holding you back, they often re-surface in moments of stress, so you should recognise them as needing solutions.

Unresolved past issues can manifest in various ways, acting as roadblocks to your empowerment. There are several signs relating to unresolved past issues, some of which may be obvious to you, whilst others are trauma-laden, and continue to silently influence your behaviour and well-being. The fact is, unresolved past issues can significantly manifest in ways that hinder your personal empowerment.

One common sign is **negative self-talk**, where individuals frequently criticise themselves or feel inadequate. This often stems from previous experiences that have eroded their confidence and self-esteem. As a result, it can lead to a pervasive **fear of failure,** because a strong aversion to taking risks or trying out new things is often deeply influenced by past mishaps or criticisms.

Additionally, many people **struggle with setting boundaries** and find it challenging to assert their personal needs or limits, due to past relationships, where boundaries were not respected. This can couple with **procrastination**, as the tendency to delay tasks or decisions might arise from unresolved traumas that create anxiety about performance or outcomes. **Emotional triggers** can also be a red flag; experiences that induce intense emotional reactions may remind you of unresolved past issues and make it difficult for you to navigate current situations rationally.

Holding onto **resentment or grudges** can further block empowerment. When individuals cling to anger or bitterness over past events or relationships, it distracts them from personal growth and forward momentum. This may lead to repeating unhealthy **relationship patterns,** reflecting unresolved issues from the past, such as dependency or avoidance behaviours. In turn, many find it **difficult to trust** others, often due to past betrayals or disappointments that hinder their ability to form supportive connections.

Another sign is the avoidance of vulnerability; individuals may find it challenging to share their feelings or seek help because past experiences have taught them to guard their emotions. This can lead to a **self-sabotaging** cycle, where engaging in behaviours that undermine your goals is rooted in deep-seated fears or beliefs formed in earlier life stages. **Chronic rumination** is another common symptom, where persistent thoughts about past events or choices prevent individuals from focusing on the present and planning for the future.

Finally, a general **lack of motivation or drive** can emerge, reflecting a sense of being stuck in old patterns and an inability to envision a positive future. Recognising these signs is essential for addressing unresolved issues and paving the way toward empowerment. Seeking support from a mental health professional or engaging in self-reflection practices can be valuable steps in working through these challenges in other to move forward.

UNRESOLVED PAST ISSUES – *SOLUTIONS*

Like all the other roadblocks we've discussed so far, there are several effective solutions to overcome them. Addressing the signs of unresolved past issues that act as roadblocks to your empowerment requires a multifaceted approach, often beginning with introspection, and a willingness to gain **self-awareness** to tap into the power within you.

⇒ The first step is to **cultivate an understanding of personal thought patterns**, particularly those rooted in negative self-talk. Engaging in practices such as journaling can help you to articulate your thoughts and feelings, serving as a means of identifying triggers and recurring themes. This process helps you to recognise the faulty narratives formed from past experiences and allows you to challenge and reframe these thoughts more positively.

⇒ **Seeking support from a mental health professional** can be crucial for those grappling with deeper emotional challenges. Therapy offers a safe space to explore unresolved issues and learn coping mechanisms. Cognitive-behavioural therapy (CBT), for instance, specifically targets maladaptive thought patterns and behaviours. It also empowers you to replace them with healthier alternatives. Through guided discussions, you can also address your fear of failure and learn to embrace risk-taking as a necessary component of growth. This will help to reshape your relationship with failure into one of learning, rather than self-condemnation.

⇒ **Setting clear boundaries** is another essential aspect of personal empowerment. You can practice assertiveness training, which helps you to articulate your needs and limits. Role-playing scenarios or seeking feedback from trusted friends can bolster one's confidence in setting and maintaining boundaries. By establishing these limits, you can begin to assert control over your life and develop a sense of control that enhances your emotional well-being.

⇒ To combat procrastination, it is beneficial to **break tasks into manageable steps** and set achievable goals. Employing time-management techniques, such as the *Pomodoro Technique*, (where you work for a short time and break for abut 25 minutes) to help you stay focused and motivated. Creating accountability by sharing goals with others, can also encourage follow-through and help you to reduce the temptation of avoiding difficult tasks.

⇒ **Developing emotional resilience** is key to navigating emotional triggers. Mindfulness practices, such as meditation or deep-breathing exercises, can ground individuals in the present moment. This enables them to respond to triggers without being overwhelmed by past associations. When feelings of resentment or grudges arise, practicing forgiveness - both for oneself and others - can liberate individuals from the emotional weight of the past. This doesn't mean condoning wrongs but rather letting go of the hold these feelings have on you is empowering.

⇒ **Building trust in relationships** can take time, but open communication and vulnerability are essential steps. Gradually allowing oneself to be vulnerable with trusted friends or family members, can help in developing a supportive network. Learning to express your feelings and needs openly fosters deeper connections, which can counteract feelings of isolation and distrust.

⇒ In order to combat self-sabotage, you may benefit from **setting clear intentions** and reflecting on your motivations and desires. Journaling about your goals, alongside your fears and doubts, can illuminate the underlying beliefs that contribute to self-sabotaging behaviours. This awareness allows you to consciously choose actions that align with your aspirations, rather than detract from them.

The following **Affirmations**, together with an **Inner Shift Journal Practice**, and a daily **Embodiment Action**, can help you solve unresolved past issues, as you delve deeper into your self-empowerment journey.

Affirmations for unresolved past issues:

1. I release the past and choose peace in the present.
2. Healing is possible, and I am worthy of it.
3. My story does not define my future.
4. I honour my pain and gently let it go.
5. Each day brings me closer to emotional freedom.

Journal Prompts:

1. What past experience or wound still lives in my mind or body?
2. How has this shaped me - and how do I want to shift that story now?
3. What would forgiveness or release feel like for me?

Embodiment Action:

Write a letter to your past self or someone involved - you don't need to send it. Burn or keep it as symbolic release.

Finally, **rekindling motivation** can be achieved through exploring and engaging in new activities that inspire your passion and joy. Setting aside time for self-care and hobbies can rejuvenate your spirit, creating a more positive outlook on the future. Also, celebrating small victories along the journey reinforces progress, and fosters a sense of accomplishment, ultimately empowering you to envision a brighter, more fulfilling path ahead. By taking the proactive steps above, you can confront unresolved issues and transform them into powerful catalysts for personal growth and empowerment.

LACK OF DISCIPLINE OR FOCUS – *ROADBLOCK*

Are you easily distracted, frequently changing priorities, or struggling to stick to a routine? Then that's a sign of lack of discipline or focus. **Lack of discipline or focus** can be a significant roadblock to your empowerment, hindering you from realizing your full potential and achieving your goals. When your discipline wavers, it often leads to a cycle of **procrastination and self-doubt**. The fact is, you may find yourself overwhelmed by aspirations but unable to follow through on the necessary steps to fulfil them. This disconnect can create feelings of inadequacy, as the gap between intention and action widens, leading to frustration and a diminished sense of your worth.

One major contributor to lack of discipline is a **crowded or chaotic environment**, both physically and mentally. There are many distractions in today's fast-paced world, whether through technology, social media, or relentless multi-tasking. For instance, the instant gratification of scrolling through social media feeds can kill your attention span and shift focus away from long-term goals. This difficulty in maintaining concentration may lead to a superficial engagement with tasks, preventing you from delving deeply enough to cultivate mastery or a sense of accomplishment. Without the ability to **concentrate on your**

objectives, you may feel aimless and demotivated, undermining your drive to pursue personal or professional aspirations.

Moreover, a **lack of clear goals** can exacerbate the struggle with discipline. When you don't define what you truly want to achieve, it becomes challenging to gather the motivation required to work toward those goals. The **absence of a roadmap** can create a sense of aimlessness, leading to a passive approach to life where opportunities are overlooked, and ambitions are left unpursued. Also, **Goal-setting practices**, including the creation of **SMART** (*Specific, Measurable, Achievable, Relevant, Time-bound*) goals, can help you establish clarity and direction, developing a more organised and disciplined approach to realising your ambitions.

Another important aspect is the relationship between **discipline and self-regulation**. The lack of self-control can manifest as an inability to resist temptations that can detract you from your goals. For example, indulging in procrastination by choosing entertainment over productive work, can reinforce a negative feedback loop. Each missed opportunity may increase your feelings of guilt or shame, and instead further diminish your self-discipline. Consequently, breaking this cycle requires cultivating self-regulation skills and developing healthier habits that support your focus and discipline.

Furthermore, **mindfulness and meditation practices** can play a crucial role in enhancing your focus and discipline. By training your mind to remain present and engaged, you can counteract distractions and improve your overall attention span. These practices not only improve your mental clarity but also help you develop greater awareness of your thoughts and emotions, making it easier to identify and control distractions that may threaten your focus. In this way, you will become more adept at recognising when you go off course, regarding your goals and can redirect your attention more effectively.

Finally, **cultivating a growth mindset** - believing that abilities can be developed through dedication and hard work - can help you overcome feelings of inadequacy associated with a lack of focus. By embracing challenges, seeking feedback, and learning from setbacks, you can build resilience and strengthen your discipline over time. This mindset encourages persistence and develops a belief in your capacity to grow, ultimately empowering you to take consistent action toward your aspirations.

In summary, a lack of discipline or focus can significantly impede your personal empowerment, as it creates barriers to taking meaningful action toward your goals. By developing an awareness of lingering distractions, setting clear objectives, developing self-regulation skills, and practicing mindfulness, you can re-establish a sense of direction and organisation in your life. Through consistent effort and a commitment to cultivating discipline, you can break free from the constraints of inaction and embark on a more empowering journey toward your aspirations.

LACK OF DISCIPLINE OR FOCUS – *SOLUTIONS*

The above is not limited to the only causes of roadblocks but by identifying these, you can at least begin to take action to overcome them. Self-reflection, seeking external support, and developing strategies to address these obstacles, are key to creating lasting change and progress, and it is also essential to awakening the power within you.

Addressing roadblocks like lack of discipline or focus, requires a comprehensive strategy that blends self-awareness, proactive planning, and the cultivation of positive habits. The journey begins with the development of self-awareness, which involves understanding one's patterns of behaviour, triggers for distraction, and the underlying motivations behind a lack of focus. Engaging in reflective practices such as journaling, can illuminate these areas, and help you to recognise when and why your discipline falters.

Once you have a clearer understanding of your habits, you can proceed to set specific, actionable goals that create a sense of direction and purpose. Utilising the **SMART criteria** - making goals *Specific, Measurable, Achievable, Relevant,* and *Time-bound* - can structure your aspirations in a way that feels manageable and motivating. Breakdowns into smaller chunks make substantial goals seem less daunting and provide clearer milestones for your success. Celebrating these small achievements along the way, reinforces positive behaviour and boosts your motivation. It also creates a cycle of accomplishment that increases more efforts.

⇒ **Time management techniques** also play a crucial role in overcoming your lack of discipline. Methods such as the *Pomodoro Technique*, which incorporates a series of focused work sessions followed by short breaks, can help you to maintain engagement and prevent burnout. By setting a timer for focused work intervals, you can train your minds to concentrate better, gradually extending your focus over time. Additionally, creating a structured daily routine ensures that essential tasks are prioritised, and you can carve out dedicated time for your work and relaxation.

⇒ **Your environment** significantly influences your discipline and focus, making it important to create a supportive workspace that minimizes distractions. This could involve decluttering a physical workspace, silencing notifications on devices, or designating specific areas for work and leisure. When you create a conducive environment, it helps to develop a mindset that is geared toward productivity, reduces temptation, and enhances your overall focus. Moreover, incorporating mindfulness practices in your life can help you develop a greater sense of presence and awareness, which strengthens your capacity to resist distractions. Techniques like meditation or deep-breathing exercises, enable you to centre your thoughts and emotions and cultivates a calmer approach to your tasks.

⇒ **Building self-discipline** also hinges on developing resilience against setbacks. Adopting a growth mindset, where you believe in your ability to improve yourself through effort, will help you to see challenges as opportunities for growth, rather than insurmountable barriers. This perspective encourages you to learn from mistakes and persist through difficulties. The result is it reinforces your commitment to your goals. Accountability can also amplify efforts in achieving discipline; by sharing your goals with friends or mentors, you invite external support and encouragement to help keep you on track.

Here are some **Affirmations** together with an **Inner Shift Journal Practice**, and a daily **Embodiment Action**, to help you deal with the *Lack of Self Discipline*, as you delve deeper into your transformational journey.

Affirmation for lack of self-discipline or focus:

1. I follow through on what matters to me.
2. I build discipline with each intentional choice.
3. My actions align with my values and goals.
4. I am capable of consistency and commitment.
5. Every day, I strengthen my self-control.

Journal Prompts:

1. Where in my life do I want to be more consistent?
2. What distractions or stories get in the way?
3. What would it feel like to show up for myself every day - even in small ways?

Embodiment Action:
Choose one tiny commitment (1-minute habit, a healthy choice, etc.) and stick to it today. Reflect on how it felt.

Finally, **self-care** plays a pivotal role in empowering you to maintain discipline. Adequate sleep, balanced nutrition, regular exercise, and moments of leisure – all contribute to optimal mental and physical well-being. When you prioritise your health, you strengthen your capacity to concentrate, manage stress, and cultivate the energy needed to stay disciplined.

In this way, the pursuit of empowerment becomes an interconnected process, where each element - the establishment of clear goals, the creation of a supportive environment, the practice of mindfulness,

awareness and commitment to self-care - works synergistically, to dissolve the roadblocks that impede your progress toward personal and professional aspirations. Through intentional effort or **mindset** and the incorporation of these strategies, you can transform your relationship with **self-discipline,** ultimately leading to a more empowered and fulfilling life.

NEGATIVE CHILDHOOD CONDITIONING – *ROADBLOCK*

In this section, we look at how early life experiences and social expectations contribute to forming your self-image, and how they impact on your personal growth and self-esteem. Self-image, the perception you have of yourself, is largely shaped by your childhood conditioning and societal norms. From the moment you were born, you are subjected to a multitude of influences that dictate how you see yourself and how you interact with the world. Parents, teachers, peers, the media, and cultural expectations - all play crucial roles in developing your self-concept.

Childhood Conditioning and Its Impact on Self-Image:

⇒ **Parental Influence**

Parents are often the primary influencers of their children's self-image. This is because their words, actions, and attitudes lay the foundation for how children perceive themselves. On one hand, positive reinforcement, encouragement, and support can help develop confidence and a strong sense of self-worth. On the other hand, criticism, neglect, or excessive control can foster insecurity, self-doubt, and low self-esteem. For example, a child who is constantly praised for their efforts, rather than just their achievements, learns that their value is intrinsic and not dependent on external validation. Conversely, a child who is frequently told they are, "not good enough" or compared to others, may internalize these negative messages, which leads to feelings of inadequacy and low self-esteem.

⇒ **Early Socialization**

Apart from parents, your extended family members, caregivers, and teachers also contribute significantly to your sense of self. The social interactions in your early childhood shape the way you understand your roles within your community. Therefore, if you grow up in an environment that develops acceptance, emotional validation, and encouragement, you are more likely to develop a positive self-image. In contrast, an upbringing marked by constant rejection, bullying, or lack of emotional support, can lead to a fragile sense of self-worth.

⇒ **Gender Conditioning**

Let's explore the above in more details and its relation to gender stereotyping. From an early age, children are conditioned to conform to gender norms that influence their self-image. Boys are often encouraged to be strong, independent, and emotionally reserved, while girls are expected to be nurturing, sensitive, and accommodating. These gendered expectations can limit self-perception and personal growth. A boy who enjoys artistic activities but is discouraged from pursuing them may feel inadequate or struggle with self-expression. Similarly, a girl who is taught to prioritise others' needs over her own, may develop a self-image based around pleasing others, rather than prioritising her own self-fulfilment.

The Role of Societal Norms in Self-Image Formation:

⇒ **Cultural Expectations**

Your culture also plays a fundamental role in shaping your self-image, by setting standards relating to beauty, success, intelligence, and behaviour. In general, societies have pre-defined ideals regarding body image, career paths, and lifestyle choices, which influence how you see yourself. For instance, in Western societies, looking thin or slim is often equated with beauty, and if you do not fit this ideal you may struggle with body dissatisfaction and low self-esteem. In fact, you may become obsessed with constantly trying to alter your body, which could lead to all kinds of phobias, fears, and a lack of self-confidence. Similarly, cultures that place a high value on academic and professional success may make you feel inadequate, if you do not meet these expectations.

⇒ **Media and Social Media Influence**

Another area in our modern world which deeply influences and perpetuates certain ideals and standards, is the media. Traditional media, such as television, movies, and magazines, often portray unrealistic and filtered versions of reality, and lead to skewed perceptions of self-worth. The rise of social media has exacerbated this issue, with platforms like Instagram and TikTok presenting highly curated versions of people's lives. This is because there is a proliferation of constant exposure to edited or photo-shopped images, popular influencers, and unrealistic beauty standards, can create feelings of inadequacy, and lead to unfavourable and unrealistic comparison of yourself to media influencers. Studies show that excessive social media use is linked to anxiety, depression, and poor self-esteem, particularly among teenagers who are still in the process of forming their self-identity. So, think about where you fit into this - are social media influencers really that important for your daily survival on this planet?

⇒ **Educational Systems**

Schooling also plays a significant role in shaping a child's self-image. Educational institutions often reinforce societal norms through grading systems, competition, and recognition of specific skills while neglecting others. Children who excel in traditional academic settings may develop a strong sense of confidence, while those who struggle with conventional subjects may internalise a belief that they are not intelligent or capable. Additionally, bullying and peer pressure in school settings can significantly impact a child's self-image. If you've experienced rejection or ridicule from your peers in the past, this may have caused deep-seated insecurities in you, which may have continued into your adult life. Unfortunately, the long-term effects of childhood conditioning and social norms have long-lasting effects.

⇒ The Long-Term Effects of Childhood Conditioning and Societal Norms

The impact of childhood conditioning and societal norms does not fade with age; rather, it continues to influence your behaviour in adulthood, your relationships, and self-perception. People who have internalized negative self-beliefs may struggle with imposter syndrome, perfectionism, and fear of failure. They may also find it difficult to set boundaries, engage in healthy relationships, or pursue their true passions. Conversely, those who were raised with encouragement and acceptance often develop resilience, confidence, and a strong sense of self-worth. They are more likely to take risks, embrace challenges, and navigate life with a sense of purpose.

NEGATIVE CHILDHOOD CONDITIONING – *SOLUTIONS*

Although childhood conditioning and societal norms play a significant role in shaping your self-image, it is possible to for you to reconstruct a more positive self-perception. To enable empowerment, certain shifts must take place consciously, to tap into your power within.

- **Self-Awareness and Reflection:** Understanding how past experiences and societal messages have shaped your self-image is the first step toward change. Journaling, therapy, and introspection can help you to identify and challenge negative self-beliefs.

- **Challenging Societal Norms:** Recognising that societal standards are often contradictory and unrealistic, will help you to define success and self-worth on your own terms. Rejecting harmful norms and embracing diversity in beauty, intelligence, and talent can develop your self-acceptance.

- **Positive Affirmations and Self-Talk:** Replacing self-critical thoughts with positive affirmations can rewire your brain to cultivate a healthier self-image. Instead of saying, *"I'm not good* enough," you can affirm, *"I am worthy and capable."*

- **Surrounding Yourself with Positive Influences:** Engaging with supportive friends, mentors, and communities can reinforce a positive self-image. Being in environments that celebrate individuality and encourage growth, helps you to counteract negative conditioning.

- **Limiting Social Media Exposure:** Reducing time spent on social media and organising your feed to include diverse, authentic representations can minimise unhealthy comparisons and improve self-esteem.

- **Therapy and Professional Support:** In cases where deep-seated self-esteem issues persist, seeking therapy or counselling can be beneficial. Cognitive-behavioural therapy (CBT) and other therapeutic approaches help you to reframe negative thought patterns and develop healthier self-perceptions.

Here are some **Affirmations**, together with an **Inner Shift Journal Practice**, and a daily **Embodiment Action**, to help you deal with overcoming negative conditioning and reconstructing self-image, as you delve deeper into your self-empowerment journey.

Affirmations for overcoming negative conditioning and reconstructing self-image:

1. *"I am free to choose my own beliefs."*
2. *"I honour my past while creating a new future."*
3. *"I am not obligated to repeat old patterns."*
4. *"I am safe to be different from how I was raised."*
5. *"I give myself permission to grow beyond my upbringing."*

Journal Prompts:

1. What beliefs, behaviours, or roles did I learn in childhood that I still carry?
2. Which of those no longer fit who I'm becoming?
3. If I could raise my inner child today, what would I teach or show them?

Embodiment Action:
Do something nurturing that your child self would've loved - art, nature, music, or play. Then make a Journal account of what came up.

In conclusion, we can agree that self-image is a complex construct, influenced by childhood conditioning and societal norms. The way we are treated as children, the messages we receive from authority figures, and the expectations imposed by society; all contribute to our self-perception. While some individuals develop a positive self-image due to nurturing environments, others struggle with self-doubt and inadequacy due to negative conditioning.

However, understanding the influences of **Affirmations, Journal Prompts and Embodiment Action** will greatly support your efforts to take control of your self-image, by challenging negative beliefs, redefining personal success, and embracing self-acceptance.

So, here are three more **Journal Prompts** to help you express yourself authentically today, by asking yourself these questions:

1. *Where have I shaped myself to meet others' expectations?*
2. *What parts of myself have I hidden or dimmed to fit in?*
3. *What would it feel like to be unapologetically me?*

In closing, I would like to challenge you to express yourself authentically today, in how you dress, speak or create. Then you must reflect on how it felt to show up as *you*.

So, as we come to the **end of Part 1 of this Book,** I have suggested thus far, that although societal norms and past conditioning can be deeply ingrained, they do not have to define your self-worth. In fact, you will experience in your self-empowerment journey, through conscious effort and **self-awareness**, you can reshape your self-image and cultivate a more fulfilling and authentic sense of self.

The following self-assessment tool, designed to evaluate your mindset at the start of your self-empowerment journey, offers a powerful approach to uncover your mind's internal drivers. It acts as both a mirror and a map, that will help you to identify your strengths, challenge limiting beliefs, and via **self-discipline**, track your personal progress.

By providing clarity and insight, at the outset, this self-assessment tool empowers you to take intentional steps toward building confidence, resilience, and purpose. My view is that in a world where personal development is key to thriving, this tool is not just helpful, but transformative as it reveals the **positive mindset** you should be striving for.

A SELF-ASSESSMENT EVALUATION OF YOUR MINDSET

Understanding your mindset at the outset of your empowerment journey is a critical step in personal growth and self-empowerment. This self-assessment tool is designed to help you reflect on your current mindset, identify areas for improvement, and take actionable steps toward cultivating a growth-oriented perspective in your life. Answer the following questions honestly and use the scoring system to evaluate your mindset.

Section 1: Beliefs About Abilities and Intelligence

1. **I believe my abilities and intelligence are fixed and cannot change significantly.**
    - Strongly Agree (1)
    - Agree (2)
    - Neutral (3)
    - Disagree (4)
    - Strongly Disagree (5)
2. **I enjoy learning new skills, even if I'm not good at them right away.**
    - Strongly Disagree (1)
    - Disagree (2)
    - Neutral (3)
    - Agree (4)
    - Strongly Agree (5)

3. **When I fail at something, I feel like it's a reflection of my inherent limitations.**
    - Strongly Agree (1)
    - Agree (2)
    - Neutral (3)
    - Disagree (4)
    - Strongly Disagree (5)

Section 2: Approach to Challenges

4. **I actively seek out challenges that push me out of my comfort zone.**
    - Strongly Disagree (1)
    - Disagree (2)
    - Neutral (3)
    - Agree (4)
    - Strongly Agree (5)
5. **When faced with a difficult task, I tend to give up easily.**
    - Strongly Agree (1)
    - Agree (2)
    - Neutral (3)
    - Disagree (4)
    - Strongly Disagree (5)
6. **I view obstacles as opportunities to learn and grow.**
    - Strongly Disagree (1)
    - Disagree (2)
    - Neutral (3)
    - Agree (4)

- Strongly Agree (5)

Section 3: Response to Feedback and Criticism

7. **I take constructive criticism personally and feel discouraged by it.**
    - Strongly Agree (1)
    - Agree (2)
    - Neutral (3)
    - Disagree (4)
    - Strongly Disagree (5)
8. **I actively seek feedback to improve myself and my work.**
    - Strongly Disagree (1)
    - Disagree (2)
    - Neutral (3)
    - Agree (4)
    - Strongly Agree (5)
9. **I believe feedback, even if negative, is valuable for my growth.**
    - Strongly Disagree (1)
    - Disagree (2)
    - Neutral (3)
    - Agree (4)
    - Strongly Agree (5)

Section 4: Persistence and Effort

10. **I believe that effort and hard work are more important than natural talent.**
    - Strongly Disagree (1)
    - Disagree (2)
    - Neutral (3)
    - Agree (4)
    - Strongly Agree (5)

11. **When I encounter setbacks, I tend to give up rather than keep trying.**
    - Strongly Agree (1)
    - Agree (2)
    - Neutral (3)
    - Disagree (4)
    - Strongly Disagree (5)

12. **I am willing to put in consistent effort, even if I don't see immediate results.**
    - Strongly Disagree (1)
    - Disagree (2)
    - Neutral (3)
    - Agree (4)
    - Strongly Agree (5)

Section 5: Attitude Toward Others' Success

13. **I feel threatened or envious when others succeed.**
    - Strongly Agree (1)

- Agree (2)
- Neutral (3)
- Disagree (4)
- Strongly Disagree (5)

14. **I am inspired by others' success and use it as motivation to improve myself.**
    - Strongly Disagree (1)
    - Disagree (2)
    - Neutral (3)
    - Agree (4)
    - Strongly Agree (5)

15. **I believe that helping others succeed does not diminish my own success.**
    - Strongly Disagree (1)
    - Disagree (2)
    - Neutral (3)
    - Agree (4)
    - Strongly Agree (5)

Scoring and Interpretation

Add up your scores for all 15 questions. **The maximum score is 75, and the minimum is 15.** Use the following ranges to interpret your results:

- **60–75: Growth Mindset**
  You have a strong growth mindset. You believe in your ability to learn, grow, and improve. You embrace challenges, persist through setbacks, and see effort as a path to mastery. Keep

nurturing this mindset and continue to seek opportunities for growth.

- **45–59: Mixed Mindset**
  You have a combination of fixed and growth mindset tendencies. While you may believe in growth in some areas, you might still hold limiting beliefs in others. Focus on identifying areas where you can shift toward a more growth-oriented perspective.

- **30–44: Developing Growth Mindset**
  You lean toward a fixed mindset but show signs of openness to growth. You may avoid challenges, fear failure, or feel threatened by others' success. Start by reframing your beliefs about abilities and effort and take small steps to embrace challenges.

- **15–29: Fixed Mindset**
  You primarily have a fixed mindset. You may believe that your abilities are static, and that effort won't lead to significant improvement. Begin by challenging these beliefs and exploring the benefits of a growth mindset. Seek out resources, such as books or workshops, to help you shift your perspective.

Action Steps to Take Based on Your Results

1. **If You Scored 60–75:**
    - Continue to challenge yourself with new goals and experiences.
    - Mentor others to reinforce your growth mindset.
    - Reflect on how your mindset has contributed to your success and share your insights with others.

2. **If You Scored 45–59:**
    - Identify specific areas where you tend to have a fixed mindset (e.g., fear of failure, avoiding challenges).
    - Practice reframing negative thoughts into growth-oriented ones.
    - Set small, achievable goals to build confidence in your ability to grow.

3. **If You Scored 30–44:**
    - Start by embracing small challenges and celebrating your effort, not just the outcome.
    - Seek feedback and view it as an opportunity to learn.
    - Surround yourself with people who have a growth mindset to inspire and motivate you.

4. **If You Scored 15–29:**
   - Begin by educating yourself about the growth mindset (e.g., read *Mindset* by Carol Dweck).
   - Challenge one fixed belief at a time (e.g., "I'm not good at this" → "I can improve with practice").
   - Take one small step outside your comfort zone each day to build resilience and confidence.

Remember, your mindset is not set in stone. With awareness, effort, and persistence, you can shift from a fixed mindset to a growth mindset. Using this self-assessment at the starting point of your self-empowerment journey helps to evaluate where you are and where you want to go. At the same time, you must bear in mind that the journey to a growth mindset is ongoing, and every step you take brings you closer to unlocking your full potential, as you learn to tap into the power within you.

Final Reflection

With awareness, effort, and persistence, you can shift from **a fixed mindset to a growth mindset**. The difference between these two states is discussed in detail in Part 2.

Use this self-assessment as a starting point to evaluate where you are and where you want to go. Remember, the journey to a **growth mindset** is ongoing, and every step you take brings you closer to unlocking your full potential.

Good luck on your journey of self-discovery and growth!

⇒ You are not broken.

⇒ You are not behind.

⇒ You are not too late.

⇒ You are awakening.

⇒ And that is enough.

PART II –
THE INNER SHIFT: THOUGHT, EMOTION § ENERGY

CHAPTER 4
Understanding Mindset

Let's be real - your mindset is either your biggest cheerleader or your loudest critic. Think about it - how often have you talked yourself out of doing something amazing because of that little voice in your head whispering, *"What if you fail?"* or *"You're not good enough"*? Probably more times than you'd like to admit. But here's the game-changer: that little voice? You can retrain it. You can teach it new lines. You can shift your mindset and *completely* transform the way you experience your life.

What is a Mindset?

Your mindset is the lens through which you see the world. It's the internal dialogue you have with yourself. It's the stories you tell yourself about who you are, what you can do, and what's possible. There are two big categories of mindset that psychologists love to talk about: **fixed** and **growth**.

- **Fixed mindset** sounds like: *"I'm just not good at this."*
- **Growth mindset** sounds like: *"I'm not good at this yet - but I can learn."*

- That one little word – **yet** - can unlock doors you didn't even know existed.

Why Your Thoughts Matter So Much

Every thought you have triggers a cascade of chemical reactions, affecting not just your mood but your immune system, physical health and long-term resilience. You must know that your emotions and thoughts affect your body at a cellular level. In her research, Dr. Candace Pert, a neuroscientist and pharmacologist, states that every thought creates chemical messengers that interact with cells throughout the body, affecting immune function, metabolism and even gene expression.

Here's a wild truth: your brain is *always* listening to you. Every time you say, *"Ugh, I'm such an idiot,"* your brain quietly takes notes. Not judging you, just updating the internal script. You say it enough times, and boom - your brain assumes it must be true.

Here is an example of real-world evidence of thought-driven biology done in a study at the University of Utah. The study examined the physiological effects of negative thought patterns in relationships, such as women in high-stress marriages had stress hormone levels compared to combat soldiers, and that their wounds healed 40% slower than those of women in healthy relationships. The study concludes that chronic negative thinking created measurable physical damage to the body. Imagine that! Your brain can filter reality, it takes in 20 million bits of sensory data per second, yet only 126 bits enter conscious awareness. As mentioned earlier in Part 1 of this book, the filter deciding what you notice is called the *Reticular Activating System (RAS)*. So, here's the plot twist: you can rewrite that script. You can flip the narrative because of the following reasons:

- The way you think shapes how you feel.
- How you feel shapes what you do.
- And what you do creates your results.

So, if you tell yourself, *"I'm unlucky,"* the *RAS* ignores opportunities and amplifies failures. If you tell yourself *"I always find solutions,"* the *RAS* highlights evidence to support that belief. So, if you want different results, you've got to start with different thoughts.

Rewiring the Internal Dialogue
Let's talk tools - because mindset shifting isn't necessarily only about chanting mantras in the mirror (though, if that works for you, go for it). It's about small, do-able changes that actually stick.

1. Catch the Thought
You can't change what you don't notice. So, the first step is becoming *aware* of your default thoughts. Start paying attention to moments when you feel discouraged, anxious, or stuck. What are you thinking

in that moment? Write it down, if you can. Seeing it on paper brings about a powerful realisation.

2. Challenge the Thought
You can reprogram the *RAS* by setting clear intentions. Write down what you want to focus on. You can even use environmental triggers; surround yourself with reminders of what you want to notice. Then repeat phrases that align your focus with your goals. Also remember that every thought follows <u>a four-stage process</u> before manifesting in the physical world: –

⇒ **Thought formation** – According to Dr. Fred Luskin of Stanford University, the human mind has 70,000 thoughts per day and 80% are negative!

⇒ **Your thoughts must be emotionally charged** – the amygdala (*the epicentre within your brain, for processing fear and rapid emotional responses, 24/7*), evaluates thoughts as either "safe" or "threatening," with 12 milliseconds, so your body releases neurotransmitters that align with that judgement – negative or positive emotion.

⇒ **Psychological response** – your facial expressions change within 0.3 seconds of a thought, and breathing rate adjusts *(shallow for stress, deep for calm)*, based on your thoughts.

⇒ **Behaviour Output** – your thoughts affect your word-choice, body language, and confidence levels, which in turn, affect how the world responds to you.

Here's an example of how thought patterns affect success in a job interview:

1. **Thought:** *"I'm not good enough."*
2. **Emotional Response:** Anxiety
3. **Physical Response:** Slumped posture, shaky voice
4. **Behavioural Output:** the interviewer subconsciously picks up on discomfort, reinforcing the self-fulfilling prophecy.

3. Choose a Better Thought

This doesn't mean pretending everything's perfect. It means finding a thought that feels believable *and* empowering. Instead of *"I'll never figure this out,"* try saying, *"This is tough, but I've figured out hard things before."* This small shift will result in a huge impact – it brings you back in control, as the latter represents conscious thought in motion.

4. Real Talk: It's a Process

Understand, I'm not sugar-coating this - it takes time. You've been thinking certain thoughts for *years*, maybe decades. They've worn grooves into your brain like tire tracks in mud, so shifting those patterns doesn't happen overnight. But every time you stop and choose a more empowering thought, you're laying down **new** tracks. You're literally **reshaping your**

brain. That's neuroplasticity at work, proving that science is on your side!

Your Turn: Quick Mindset Reboot

Here's a challenge for mental reprogramming protocol over a 30-day period that you can try: This method is based on research led by Dr. Shad Helmstetter, Stanford psychologists and cognitive neuroscientists.

This mental reprogramming challenge could be tried over 3 phases as follows:

PHASE 1: **Thought Awareness** - (1-7 days)
ACTION: Carry a tally counter and click each time you notice a negative thought. The goal is not elimination – it is aimed at **awareness.**

PHASE 2: **Pattern Interruption** - (8-14 days)
ACTION: Use the snap-back technique (e.g. Snap a rubber band on your wrist when a negative thought arises).
Say the word *"cancel"* aloud and replace it with a positive thought.

PHASE 3: **Conscious Construction** – (15-30 days)
Morning: 5 minutes of visualisation
Midday: Check-in meditation
Evening: Gratitude Journaling

From Survival Mode to Power Mode

Most of us move through life on autopilot - reacting instead of intentionally responding, surviving instead of truly living. But understanding mindset is the first step to shifting from default mode to power mode. This shift isn't about toxic positivity or pretending everything is perfect; it's about reclaiming your role as the conscious creator of your experience. It is also best understood when the principles of the **Self-Empowerment Excellence Model (SEEM)**© are applied to an understanding of mindset.

Through **self-awareness**, you begin to notice your thought patterns - how you interpret challenges, how you speak to yourself, and where you may be holding yourself back. With **self-discipline**, you commit to interrupting those automatic reactions and choosing responses that align with your values and vision. And by cultivating a **positive mindset**, you learn to view life through a lens of growth, resilience, and possibility. You get to take back the steering wheel. You get to decide how you meet your moments, how you shape your narrative, and how you rise, again and again.

Final Thoughts

You've just learned that your thoughts are not random - they are the foundation of your emotions, actions, and destiny. By learning to direct them **consciously,** you can reshape your perception and alter the trajectory of your life.

You are the architect of your reality! **Challenge negative thoughts** and replace them with those that are empowering, and believable. Over time, your attitude to thinking will change. Remember, every major breakthrough in history - from Edison's inventions to Beethoven composing while deaf, came from individuals who mastered their thoughts.

CHAPTER 5
The Mindset Shift – Transforming Your Thought Patterns

There comes a moment in every journey when the most powerful transformation is not external, but internal - a quiet revolution within the mind. That moment, subtle yet profound, is the **mindset shift.**

In the last chapter, we explored how your thoughts are a sacred ground - shaping your self-perception, colouring your worldview, and influencing how you rise or retreat. Within the mind lies both limitation and liberation, and the key to choosing empowerment begins with **self-awareness**: becoming conscious of the beliefs and inner narratives that drive you.

From there, **self-discipline** becomes the commitment to interrupt old thought patterns, to redirect the inner dialogue, and to consistently choose thoughts that align with your growth. And it is through a **positive mindset** that you begin to reframe challenges as opportunities, fear as a teacher, and doubt as a doorway to deeper trust.

The invitation for change and transformation is underpinned via the **Self-Empowerment Excellence**

Model **(SEEM)** ©, which is to consciously move from self-doubt to self-empowerment, from fear to faith, from fixed patterns to a mindset rooted in resilience, purpose, and possibility.

Understanding the Power of Mindset

In both professional development and personal evolution, the concept of "mindset" has become central - and rightfully so. Your mindset is the internal architecture that determines how you respond to challenges, how you relate to others, and how you navigate your highest calling.

The late Dr. Carol Dweck, a renowned psychologist, and expert about Mindset, introduced the concept of **fixed vs. growth mindsets**:

- A **fixed mindset** believes that talents, intelligence, and potential are static. It says, *"This is who I am, and I cannot change."*

- A **growth mindset** believes that with effort, openness, and resilience, we can expand beyond our perceived limitations. It whispers, *"I am always becoming."*

Spiritual wisdom echoes this truth: *"Be transformed by the renewing of your mind."* (Romans 12.2). This

Biblical verse means growth begins where the soul aligns with truth - and truth always affirms possibility.

The Inner Conversation Shapes the Outer Reality

Thoughts are not just fleeting ideas - they are energetic seeds. What you plant in the soil of your mind, you will inevitably harvest in your life. If the voice within says, *"I'm not enough,"* the world around you will seem to confirm it. If the voice says, *"I am capable, and I trust the process,"* doors begin to open.

A transformed life begins with a transformed dialogue. As professionals, leaders, creators, and spiritual beings, we must police our thoughts with intention. We must learn to silence the noise of scarcity, perfectionism, and comparison - and instead cultivate the quiet strength of belief, patience, and possibility.

Cultivating a Growth Mindset: A Spiritual and Professional Practice

The journey toward a growth mindset is not an intellectual exercise alone - it is a sacred discipline. Here are six intentional practices to help you align with it:

1. Awareness: Witness Without Judgment

Observe your thoughts gently and without shame. Notice when limiting beliefs arise. They are to be found in language that states:

- *"I'll never be good at this."*
- *"They're better than I am."*
- *"What if I fail?"*

Do not fight these thoughts - simply witness them like distant weather patterns and let them drift without engaging. You do not need to battle your mind, just stop giving it your energy. The quieter your mind, the clearer your signal. Light transforms darkness by illuminating it, not resisting it. Just know that in awareness, there is power.

2. Reframe Challenges as Sacred Assignments

Every obstacle carries within it a divine opportunity. A growth mindset sees setbacks not as signs of failure, but as invitations to expand. Ask yourself: *"What is this moment here to teach me?"* When the ego sees a wall, the spirit sees a doorway.

3. Speak with Intention

Words are spells, whether spoken aloud or silently within. Begin to use affirming, empowering language, not as empty platitudes, but as declarations of truth.

Try embodying your language with statements like these:

- *"I am learning and evolving every day."*
- *"I give myself permission to grow."*
- *"I trust the process unfolding within me."*

Speak to yourself as someone you are responsible for nurturing – **you!**

4. Embrace the Power of "Yet"

In professional and spiritual growth, perfection is a myth. No one is perfect but the language of striving in the process, is the truth. If you catch yourself thinking, *"I'm not confident,"* add one sacred word: **yet.** *"I'm not confident yet. But I am growing."* The word "Yet" seems to open up the space for grace.

5. Surround Yourself with Expansive Energy

Here's a fact - Energy is contagious, and that being so, you should seek communities, mentors, and environments that reflect the mindset you wish to embody. Be in the presence of people who believe in becoming, who are not afraid to begin again, and who lead with humility and hope. Your mindset will rise to match the company it keeps.

6. Integrate Reflection and Gratitude

Take time to reflect on your journey. Growth is not always visible in the moment, but it reveals itself in hindsight. When you recognise growth, you should express gratitude. I know the word 'gratitude' gets mentioned a lot, but it's not just saying *'thanks"*, it's a mindset, a habit, a quiet practice that can truly reshape how we live and how we feel.

Gratitude is simply the act of noticing and appreciating the good in your life. And not just the big wins, but the little, everyday moments too. It's saying, *"I see this. I value this. I don't take it for granted."* And in going forward, you should ask yourself these questions:

- *Where have I stretched this week?*
- *What thought patterns have I released?*
- *What small wins can I honour?*

What's beautiful about gratitude is that science backs it up. The truth is, expressing gratitude regularly and consciously has been linked to better sleep, stronger relationships, lower stress, even reduced symptoms of depression. Research published in *Behavioural Brain Research,* led by Dr. Robert Emmons in 2015, the world's foremost scientific expert on gratitude, revealed that individuals who engage in daily gratitude practices demonstrate a 23% elevation in baseline serotonin levels, helping emotional regulation, such as reducing anxiety and improving cognitive control.

In fact, it when you practice expressing gratitude regularly, you're literally training your brain to look for the good. You are rewiring your mindset toward positivity and presence. It doesn't mean ignoring pain or pretending life is perfect. It means creating space for hope and joy, even when things are tough. In other words, gratitude anchors growth. It tells your spirit: *Keep going. You're on the right path.*

The Soul of Empowerment

At its essence, a growth mindset is an act of spiritual alignment. It is remembering that you are not a finished product, but a living process - fluid, dynamic, and evolving. Transformation does not come from trying harder. It comes from believing deeper. It comes from returning to your inner truth: that you were made to grow, to rise, and to shine.

When you change the way you think, you don't just change your life - you change the way you experience yourself in the world. You become not only more effective and resilient, but more whole.

Let this be your mantra: *"I am not stuck. I am shifting. I am not finished. I am becoming."* And in that sacred becoming, you will find your power.

CHAPTER 6
Coming Home to the Now

We live in a culture that glorifies hustle - where worth is often measured by output, and rest feels like a luxury that we must earn. You answer emails while eating lunch, multi-task on your morning walk, and feel guilty when your to-do list isn't complete. But here's the truth no one told you: you are not behind, you are not late, and your right to rest is not something you have to prove.

It is for this reason that applying the principles of the **Self-Empowerment Excellence Model (SEEM)**©, to the power of presence, encapsulates the very essence of what it means to be present. For example, **Self-awareness** allows you to recognize these ingrained patterns - the pressure to perform, the fear of slowing down and to question whether they truly serve you. **Self-discipline** then becomes the quiet strength to choose differently: to pause, to breathe, to protect your peace, even when the world demands your pace. And with a **positive mindset**, you reclaim rest not as a weakness, but as wisdom - as a radical act of self-respect. Presence then becomes your resistance. It says, *"My peace matters more than my productivity."*

Beneath the ever-present noise is stillness. Behind the resulting chaos is clarity. But within you, is a quiet space, untouched by fear or frenzy. That space is presence. In a world that pulls you into the past or pushes you toward the future, the most powerful gift you can offer yourself is to return to the **now** – fully, gently and intentionally.

What Does It Mean to Be Present?

To be present is not simply to pause or take a deep breath - though those are beautiful doorways. Presence means to **live awake.** To become fully aware of what is happening within and around you, without rushing to escape or control it.

Presence is not about doing nothing. It's about doing one thing with your whole heart, being aware of the moment. In other words, it could look this this in practice:

- ⇒ Drinking your coffee whilst *actually* tasting it!
- ⇒ Listening to your friend without prematurely thinking of your reply
- ⇒ Noticing the breeze on your skin
- ⇒ Taking three deep breaths before you reach for your phone
- ⇒ Its saying: *"I'm here, and here is enough."*

Being present is also the art of showing up for your own life, moment by moment.

- It's hearing your own voice underneath the world's expectations.
- It's noticing the sensation of sunlight on your skin or the tension in your shoulders.

- It's catching the way your thoughts drift when you're uncomfortable and lovingly guiding them back.

But know that presence is not perfection – it' is simply *attention* with compassion, and presence is power.

Why Presence Matters in the Journey of Self-Empowerment

Presence is where your **real power** lives. Presence exists neither in yesterday's regrets, nor in tomorrow's fears. Presence is here - **now.** And when you're present, this is what happens: You're no longer reacting from old patterns, you can hear the quiet wisdom of your inner voice and you have the clarity to choose, instead of being pulled by habit.

Presence gives you space to shift, space to respond rather than react and space to *breathe before you believe* whatever the world throws at you. In this space, healing begins. Growth takes root, and self-empowerment becomes not just a concept, but a **lived experience.**

How the Mind Resists the Now

Let's be honest: the present moment is simple, but it's not always easy. The mind often prefers to dwell on the past - replaying mistakes, dissecting conversations, or clinging to old stories. At times, it leaps ahead into the future by your worrying, overthinking, or trying to control what hasn't yet happened. This is normal, and it's the mind's way of seeking safety. However, true safety which is deep, and grounded peace, comes when we reconnect with the only thing we truly have: **this moment.**

Practices to Return to Presence

Whenever you find yourself slipping or being distracted from the quiet wisdom of your inner voice, you can return to presence. You don't have to escape your life to find peace because presence meets you exactly where you are. Here are some grounded, gentle ways to cultivate presence:

1. Conscious Breath

Know that your breath is a sacred anchor and you can practice this any time, and anywhere, because breath is what we have always that sustains us.
Take three slow, intentional breaths.
Inhale: *"I am here."*
Exhale: *"This moment is enough."*

You can repeat this anytime you feel disconnected, in order to return to presence.

2. Sensory Awareness

To bring you back to awareness, you should pause from whatever you're doing. Then name what you notice, based on one thing you see, one thing you hear and one thing you feel. This brings you back to the body and out from your spiralling thoughts.

3. Single-Tasking with Intention

Whether you're washing dishes, sending an email, or walking, do it with full attention. Let it become a meditation - a conscious action. In this way, presence is able to turn the mundane into a sacred ritual.

4. Body Scan

*[**Advice:** Remember that before doing any practice that relates to closing your eyes, you should always ensure that you are not driving or operating any machinery or moving equipment].*

For this body scan, you must close your eyes. Bring awareness from the crown of your head down to your toes. Notice where there is tension and where there is ease. Simply notice, without trying to change anything. Your body is a wise teacher of what your soul needs. *(For a full-length awareness meditation practice, please go to Chapter 11).*

5. Pause Before Response

A wise person once said that a sensible code to live by is being in control of your response in all conversations - especially the difficult ones. Simple and profound, the advice is to pause before responding. This is because a single breath can shift your words from reaction to wisdom.

Presence and Spiritual Alignment

From a spiritual perspective, presence is where we meet the Divine. Whether you call it Source, God, the Universe, or simply Life-force, its energy is always found *here*, never elsewhere. This is because, the past is memory - the future is imagination and the now is where the sacred resides.

Presence is how we honour this moment as holy. When we live in presence, we stop chasing and start receiving. We stop striving and start aligning. Life flows more freely, not because it gets easier, but because we meet it with greater grace.

Presence as a Spiritual Practice

The more present you become, the more alive you feel. Life doesn't happen "out there." It unfolds here - in each breath, each word, each step and glance. This moment is the only place where transformation is possible - the only space where healing, creation, and connection truly exist. Our **Self-Empowerment**

Excellence Model (SEEM),© when applied to the power of presence, confirms that the journey to awaken the power within truly lies in the inner and equitable workings of a triangular relationship between self-awareness, self-discipline and a positive mindset.

In other words, to embrace presence is to cultivate **self-awareness**: to notice your inner world with clarity, to observe without judgment, and to recognise the subtle patterns shaping your experience. It's in this awareness that we begin to remember who we are, beneath the noise.

But presence also calls for **self-discipline** - the conscious choice to slow down, to resist distraction, and to keep returning to the now, especially when the world urges you to rush past it. Presence becomes a daily practice, not of perfection, but of choosing alignment; again, and again.

When grounded in a **positive mindset**, this practice becomes an invitation - not a task. You begin to trust the wisdom of the moment, to see each pause as purposeful, and each breath as a bridge back to yourself.

Embracing presence as a spiritual practice invites us into deeper communion - with ourselves, with others, and with something greater than us. It becomes less about doing and more about *being* - a sacred returning to what is real, right now.

The Inner Shift: From Noise to Knowing

In the quiet space and stillness of now, you can hear the whisper of your soul: *You are already enough. You are already whole. You are already home.* That is the essence of self-empowerment - not to become someone else, but to return to who you truly are, beneath the noise.

Reflection: A Presence Journal

Here is a daily reflection practice for you to pause and become aware of your presence. Each day, pause and make a Journal entry of the following:

- *"What moment today brought me peace?"*
- *"When did I feel most disconnected - and why?"*
- *"What am I noticing in this moment, right now?"*

This simple reflection trains your mind to seek presence instead of distraction.

A Presence Pause

Here's something you can do right now, wherever you are to return to presence:

⇒ Stop what you're doing.
⇒ Take a deep breath in.
⇒ Feel your feet on the ground.

⇒ Gently ask yourself, *"What's real in this moment? What do I notice?"*

That's presence.

So, in summary, presence is not a destination. It's a returning; again, and again. Every breath, every pause, every moment you choose to come back, you are empowering yourself, because real empowerment isn't about becoming someone else. It's about waking up to the truth that **you were never lost**. You simply forgot how powerful it is to be fully... here.

Let this be your quiet revolution: ***To live awake. To love from the centre. To come home to now.***

CHAPTER 7
Emotional Intelligence: Honouring Your Feelings as Guides

Many of us were taught to silence our emotions - to hide what felt like, *"too much"* or to pretend we were fine when our hearts were aching. Here's the truth - suppressing an emotion doesn't make it disappear. It buries it deeply within the body, where it lingers, eventually surfacing as anxiety, exhaustion, disconnection, or even illness. However, by applying the principles of the **Self-Empowerment Excellence Model (SEEM)**©, we can begin to appreciate how the triangular model complements the development of emotional intelligence, and leads you to a position of strength, courage and wisdom.

Emotional intelligence begins with **self-awareness** - the willingness to feel what's present without judgment, to meet your inner world with honesty and compassion. Your emotions are not flaws or failures; they are messengers, sacred signals pointing you toward what is true, what is unresolved, and what longs to be healed or honoured.

Through **self-discipline**, you build the capacity to pause, reflect, and respond, rather than react, and to sit with discomfort, rather than avoid it. And with a **positive mindset**, you begin to see emotions not as obstacles, but as powerful guides leading you into deeper wholeness.

To be truly empowered is not to control your emotions, but to trust them - to listen, learn, and grow through them. This is emotional intelligence in action: the courage to feel, the strength to stay present, and the wisdom to choose growth.

What really Is Emotional Intelligence?

Emotional intelligence (often called EQ), is the ability to recognise, understand, and manage your emotions - while also being able to connect with and respond to the emotions of others. It's a blend of self-awareness, empathy, and mature self-regulation. But it's also more than that.

Spiritually, emotional intelligence is a form of wisdom. It's the inner knowing that every feeling has something to teach you.

>Your **anger** reveals your boundaries.
>Your **sadness** speaks of what you've loved and lost.
>Your **fear** shows you where safety matters.
>Your **joy** points to what your soul was made for.

Why This Matters on the Path of Self-Empowerment

You cannot become fully empowered while rejecting the most human parts of yourself. Emotions are **energy in motion** - they are not to be judged or labelled as *"good"* or *"bad."* They are part of your guidance system. To honour your feelings is to reclaim your wholeness. It's to say: *"Every part of me is worthy of compassion. Every part of me belongs."* When you stop running from your emotions, you begin to lead your life from a place of alignment, rather than avoidance.

How to build Emotional Intelligence

Here are five foundational steps to develop emotional intelligence with spiritual depth and practical wisdom.

1. Feel Without Fixing

When a difficult emotion arises - like grief, envy, shame, or anger - your first instinct may be to numb, solve, or suppress it. Instead of doing so, pause - you should *breathe* and *feel*. Then ask yourself:

- *Where is this emotion showing up in my body?*
- *What does it want me to notice?*
- *Can I sit with it without rushing to fix it?*

Sitting with emotion is not weakness, it's strength. You become stronger not by pushing it away, but by expanding your capacity to hold it.

2. Name It to Navigate It

There's not only importance but also power in naming what you feel. The moment you say, *"I'm feeling overwhelmed,"* or *"I feel left out,"* or *"This triggered sadness in me,"* you've already created space between you and the emotion. You are not the emotion. You are the awareness *of* it. The reality is, language brings clarity, and clarity brings choice.

3. Trace the Root, Not Just the Surface

Often, what we feel on the surface is just the tip of something deeper. For example, here is a scenario with a superficial feeling:

- **Surface:** *"I'm irritated with my partner."*
- **Root:** *"I feel unseen. I feel like my needs aren't valued."*

When this happens, you should try asking these questions:

- *When have I felt this before?*
- *What does this remind me of?*
- *What's the deeper wound beneath this reaction?*

This level of insight empowers healing, and it is not just short-term relief.

4. Express with Responsibility and Compassion

Emotional intelligence is not about bottling up or exploding. It's about expressing how you feel with honesty and care - especially in relationships. Use "I" statements:

- *"I felt hurt when I didn't hear back from you."*
- *"I'm feeling anxious, and I need some reassurance."*

You don't need to be perfect. You just need to be real, and respectful. It's not exposing your weakness or vulnerability either. It's leadership - from the inside out.

5. Practice Self-Compassion as Emotional First Aid

But what is self-compassion? Dr. Kristin Neff, an expert researcher on this subject, defines self-compassion as having three key components:

1. **Self-kindness** – treating yourself like you'd treat a friend.
2. **Common humanity** – realising you're not alone in your struggles.
3. **Mindfulness** – observing your pain without exaggerating or suppressing it.

It's not about letting yourself off the hook or giving up accountability; it's about giving yourself the grace to be a work in progress.

I learnt this lesson some time ago. I remember a time when I missed a major deadline. I was beating myself up, spiralling into that inner voice which says; *"You're so irresponsible. You always mess things up."* But then I paused, took a breath and asked myself: *"What would I say to a friend in this exact situation?"* The answer? *"Hey, you've been carrying a lot. You made a mistake. But this doesn't define you. You are allowed to regroup and keep going."* That simple shift didn't erase the consequences, but it stopped the emotional bleeding. It gave me room to respond instead of reacting. That's the power of self-compassion.

So, when you're emotionally overwhelmed, try saying this to yourself:

- *"It's okay to feel this."*
- *"This feeling is valid and temporary."*
- *"I'm doing the best I can right now."*

Here's the truth: You don't have to be perfect to be proud of who you are. You don't have to earn your worth by never messing up. You're already worthy. Faults and all!

Here's an important take-away, Self-compassion regulates the nervous system, softens judgment, and helps you come back to centre. It reminds you that you are safe, loved, and capable of moving through whatever arises.

Emotions as Sacred Messengers

Every emotion carries divine information. You should understand that your feelings are not here to harm you - they are here to guide you. When you learn to honour them, you unlock a deeper intuition. You begin to live from the inside out. You stop performing. You stop people-pleasing. You stop abandoning yourself for the sake of peace. Instead, you listen. You honour. You respond with grace and strength.

Reflection: A Gentle Emotional Check-In

Whenever you are ambivalent about your feelings, you can use this short practice to increase your emotional awareness:

- *What am I feeling right now?*
- *Where is it in my body?*
- *What might this emotion be trying to teach or show me?*
- *What do I need in this moment - comfort, movement, expression, silence?*

It does not have to be long hours of introspection, just one minute of honest reflection can shift everything.

The Heart of Empowerment

In summary, Emotional intelligence is not a luxury - it's a necessity for authentic, lasting empowerment. When you become the steward of your emotional world, you begin to lead your life from the heart, not the wound. Let your feelings guide you - not by controlling your path, but by illuminating it. The fact is, an empowered human being isn't one who never feels deeply, but one who knows how to walk through emotions with dignity, softness, and strength.

So, let your heart speak - and more important, learn to listen.

CHAPTER 8
The Energy Within – Aligning with Higher Vibrations

Everything is energy. Your thoughts, emotions, words, and presence all carry a frequency - each one either elevates or drains, expands or limits. We are not merely physical beings in a material world; we are energetic beings, constantly radiating, receiving, and shaping reality through vibration. We align our energy with higher vibrations by incorporating the **Self-Empowerment Excellence Model (SEEM)**© principles and its application.

On a practical level, we apply these by cultivating **self-awareness**, by noticing how our internal state affects what we attract and experience. With **self-discipline**, we choose practices, habits, and thoughts that raise our vibration rather than lower it. And through a **positive mindset**, we align with possibility, abundance, and higher states of being.

This isn't just wishful thinking - it's energetic alignment. When we live from this place, we move with intention, embody empowerment, and consciously create a reality that reflects our highest self. This is the energy within - activated, aligned, and in resonance with the life we are meant to live.

Understanding Vibration and Frequency

If you want to be crystal clear about how vibration and frequency works, imagine yourself as **a radio tower.** As a radio tower, you are always transmitting a signal - through your mood, your beliefs, your intentions, and your actions. That **signal attracts experiences and people** who match its frequency. This isn't magic, it's **resonance.**

High-frequency states like love, gratitude, compassion, clarity, and joy tend to generate openness, ease, and inspiration. **Lower-frequency states** like fear, resentment, shame, or chronic stress often leads to constriction, confusion, and disconnection. You are not "wrong" for feeling low-vibration emotions - they are part of the human experience, but staying there in the long-term, disconnects you from your power. The question is not; *'How can I never feel low again?'* Instead, it should be, *'How quickly can I return to alignment?'*

Why Energy Awareness Is Self-Empowerment

The more attuned you become to your energy, the more you realize that external circumstances don't define your state - you do. You can choose calm, when others choose chaos. You can embody love when judgment is loud, and you can also stay rooted when everything around you is wavering. That is energetic mastery. It is spiritual leadership, as well as self-empowerment in action.

Signs You're Out of Alignment

We all drift sometimes, but awareness is how we find our way back. Here are subtle signs which show that your energy may be out of alignment:

- You feel anxious, heavy, or irritable for no clear reason.
- You're reactive or easily overwhelmed by others' emotions.
- You feel disconnected from your purpose or intuition.
- You procrastinate, self-sabotage, or overthink.
- You sense you're not living in integrity with your values.

These are not failures - they are signals, and when honoured, they become your invitations to recalibrate – to return from your drifting and shift your vibration.

How to Shift Your Energy Intentionally

You do not need to wait for a perfect moment to shift your vibration. Energy moves when you move - mentally, emotionally, or physically. Below are some powerful steps to help you return to alignment:

1. Cleanse Your Inner Environment

Your thoughts are energetic fuel, so you should notice **what** you're saying to yourself. Are your words loving? Uplifting? True? If not, you should replace draining inner dialogue with intentional affirmation:

- *"I am grounded in peace."*
- *"I am available for clarity."*
- *"I release what no longer serves me."*

Remember, your words are like spells; you send them out with energy, and they manifest what has been said. Therefore, you should speak wisely!

2. Move Your Body, Move Your Energy

Did you know that stagnant energy lives in the body? You tend to feel this when there is a cramp, stiffness, and stuck energy can also feel like pain and discomfort. Let your energy flow freely, by doing gentle movements like stretching, dancing, walking, and even shaking out tension. These help your energy to circulate and release. Let your body guide you toward freedom. Let movement become a medicine and you will notice how energised you feel after moving your body.

3. Ground into Nature's Rhythm

It's a fact that nature is the original energetic healer. So, you should make the most of enjoying the outdoors. Go out into your garden, or in a park - take off your shoes and put your feet directly on the earth. By doing so you are actually drawing in natural, freely available energy! Become mindful of a whole environment of energetic healing opportunities wherever you are. Sit and watch a sunset. Feel the wind. Listen to birdsong. With this awareness, when your energy feels chaotic, the natural world will remind you how to come back into harmony - effortlessly and without force.

4. Nourish with Stillness and Silence

Silence is not emptiness - it's sacred space. Make time for quiet reflection, meditation, or simply breathing without distraction; as often as you can. In stillness, you can feel what you've been avoiding. You can hear the subtle whispers of your soul. This is where clarity rises.

5. Surround Yourself with Elevated Energy

Here is a fact - energy is contagious! Notice how people behave in certain environments – whilst in a party or bar, a solemn ceremony, a restaurant or at a gathering of any kind. The energy in every individual environment has an impact on you and consequently affects your behaviour. Therefore, choose your environments, content, music, and people who inspire and uplift you, carefully.

Ask yourself:

- *Does this support my highest self?*
- *Does this expand or drain me?*
- *Do I leave feeling more connected or more lost?*

The answer to these questions will help to clarify when you need to choose the environments that align, and when to release what dims or does not serve you.

Raising Your Vibration Isn't About Perfection

Let's be clear - raising your vibration doesn't mean you'll never face hard days or emotional waves. You are a human being and are meant to feel, but alignment means you don't stay stuck. **You feel, you process, and then you re-align.** And in that sacred rhythm, you become a powerful energetic presence - not only for yourself, but for others.

Daily Energy Tune-Up (Simple Practice)

Take five minutes each morning or evening to check in:

1. *What is my current energetic state?*
2. *What may have influenced it today?*
3. *What simple action could help me realign?* (E.g., journal, stretch, drink water, pause, release a thought.)

This practice strengthens awareness, which is the beginning of transformation.

Reflection Reminders - You Are the Source

⇒ You are not waiting to be empowered by life.

⇒ You are the source.

⇒ You are the frequency.

⇒ You are the vibration that shapes every moment.

Finally, when you align with your truth, your integrity, and your inner peace - you become magnetic. You stop chasing and instead, start attracting. You stop forcing and start flowing. This is not selfish. It is sacred stewardship of your energy, and it is one of the most loving, empowering things you can offer to yourself and the world.

PART III – EMBODIMENT OF POWER AND PURPOSE

CHAPTER 9
Embodying Confidence – Trusting Yourself Deeply

True confidence isn't loud - it doesn't seek to prove, perform, or posture. It emanates from within: grounded, calm, and quietly powerful. In other words, you no longer rely on the world to give you permission. You move from a place of inner authority; knowing that you are whole, capable and worthy. This is not something you must earn; it is something you remember. Confidence is not the absence of fear; it is the presence of trust - trust in yourself, your intuition, your voice, and your path.

This kind of trust is cultivated through **self-awareness,** recognizing your patterns, strengths, and truth without judgment. It is strengthened by **self-discipline,** the daily practice of honouring your values and showing up for yourself, even when it's hard. And it is sustained by a **positive mindset** that chooses growth over doubt and self-belief over external validation. When these **Self-Empowerment Excellence Model (SEEM)**© pillars align, you no longer wait for the world's permission. You lead from inner authority - a deep knowing that you are whole, capable, and worthy.

Confidence, then, is not something you chase or earn. It's something you remember and choose - moment by moment.

What Is Embodied Confidence?

Most people confuse confidence with an image of bravado, but embodied confidence isn't about being perfect or always knowing the answer. It's about feeling rooted in yourself, even when things are uncertain. This is because you trust -

- That your voice matters.
- That you can navigate the unknown.
- That your presence is enough.

Embodied confidence is a spiritual posture, because it says: *"I belong here. I carry wisdom. I walk with my soul, not my ego."* It's not about being above others - it's about no longer shrinking beneath them.

Why Confidence Is a Spiritual Practice

When you reclaim your confidence, you're not just shifting mindset - you're restoring **divine alignment**. You begin to live in integrity with who you truly are - not the version the world moulded, but the version your soul always remembered. This kind of confidence is sacred because it liberates others, too. Your self-trust gives them permission to trust themselves. Your voice becomes a ripple in the collective awakening.

What Diminishes Confidence?

Our behaviour, based on some of the roadblocks stated in Part 1 of this book, has alerted us to naming the kinds of behaviour that hinders our development of self-confidence. However, before we can rebuild confidence, we must lovingly name what drains it:

- Chronic self-doubt or overthinking
- People-pleasing and over-apologizing
- Perfectionism and fear of failure
- Comparing yourself to others
- Outsourcing validation or waiting for permission

These behaviours often begin as 'protection,' but they become cages. And the key to your freedom is not in fixing yourself, but in **trusting yourself more deeply**, and taking steps to solving the problems of these roadblocks to confidence, as already highlighted in Chapters 1 to 3.

Foundations of Unshakable Self-Trust

Here are five foundational shifts to help you build embodied confidence from the inside out:

1. Keep Small Promises to Yourself

Confidence grows when you become someone you can count on. Each time you keep a commitment to yourself, whether it's resting when you said you would, finishing something you started, or setting a boundary; you can reinforce this inner message: *"I trust myself to follow through."* Start small. Build slowly, and remember, it's consistency over perfection.

2. Make Decisions from Alignment, Not Anxiety

It might surprise you to know that confident people don't always *know* the right answer. They simply learn to trust their own clarity. So, when faced with choices, you must pause and ask these questions:

- *Does this align with my values?*
- *Is this a true yes or a fear-based, yes?*
- *If I trusted myself fully, what would I choose?*

Trusting your intuition is a form of divine leadership. The more you honour it, the stronger it becomes.

3. Release the Need for External Approval

Seeking validation is a human thing to do, but living for it, is definitely disempowering. Here are questions that a person with confidence would ask:

- *Can I validate myself first?*
- *Can I make peace with being misunderstood?*
- *Can I belong to myself, even if others don't agree?*

Remember, you don't need to convince the world - you just need to **stand with your soul**.

4. Let Your Body Lead the Way

Confidence is felt physically. Try this - Stand tall. Open your chest. Breathe deeply. Relax your jaw. Make eye contact. Feel the shift? Your posture, breath, and movement will send powerful signals to your nervous system and to others that say, *"I am safe. I am here. I am grounded."* Use your body to return to your power.

5. Celebrate Progress, Not Perfection

You don't need to have it all figured out to be confident. You only need to honour the *courage to keep showing up.* Acknowledging the small wins is like celebrating them – the kind of wins that include the boundary you set, the truth you spoke, the idea you followed through on, and the moment you stayed present, instead of spiralling. Most important, you must remember that confidence grows with self-recognition. So, you must learn to witness and affirm your own evolution.

A Soul-Cantered Confidence Practice

Take a few quiet minutes to journal or reflect on the following questions:

1. *Where in my life am I already confident?*
2. *Where am I currently outsourcing trust?*
3. *What does it feel like when I fully trust myself?*
4. *What would shift if I embodied that trust today?*

The answers will help you centre your confidence and allow self-recognition as you grow and acknowledge your progress. Let this be your practice: not chasing confidence but **becoming** it.

You Are Worthy of Your Own Trust

So, now the message is clear - confidence is not something you *"achieve."* It is something you reclaim, by remembering that the truth is encapsulated in the following statements:

- You are capable of hard things.
- Your intuition is wise.
- You are allowed to take up space.
- You don't need to prove anything.
- You are already enough.

When you begin to trust yourself deeply, life meets you differently - Doors open - Voices soften - Miracles will unfold because the world mirrors the energy you hold within.

So, in summary, walk as if you belong. Speak as if your words are sacred. Lead as if your soul chose this exact path - because it did. You don't have to earn your place.

You already are the embodiment of confidence.

CHAPTER 10
Boundaries and Integrity – Protecting Your Peace

As you continue progressing on your self-empowerment journey, you begin to realise a powerful truth: you were not created to be everything to everyone. Through **self-awareness**, you come to understand that betraying your own soul for the sake of keeping the peace is not true harmony - it's self-abandonment. There comes a pivotal moment in this journey when you must fully acknowledge that your energy is sacred, your time is valuable, and your peace is non-negotiable.

This level of clarity calls for **self-discipline** - the consistent, courageous practice of honouring your limits, saying *no* when needed, and choosing alignment over approval. Boundaries, then, are not walls to keep others out; they are bridges that keep *you* connected to your truth, your purpose, and your well-being.

Additionally, with a **positive mindset**, you shift your perspective on boundaries from guilt or fear to empowerment and self-respect. You begin to see that peace isn't a luxury - it's a necessity. Because without peace, there is no clarity. And without clarity, your power begins to dim. But when you apply the **Self-Empowerment Excellence Model (SEEM)**© to this truth, you begin to realise that when you live with awareness, discipline, and a mindset rooted in self-worth, you protect the light within you - and that light becomes unstoppable.

What really Are Boundaries?

Boundaries are clear lines that define what is okay for you and what is not - emotionally, physically, mentally, spiritually, or energetically. They are not punishments. They are **protections**, and they communicate the following:

- What you are available for.
- What you are no longer willing to accept.
- What you need to stay true to yourself.

Boundaries are how you honour your energy, not just emotionally, but spiritually. They are not just acts of courage; they are acts of self-respect.

Why Boundaries Matter for Empowerment

Boundaries really matter because living without boundaries can seem like you are:

- Constantly overwhelm or burnout.
- Saying yes when your body says no.
- Feeling resentful, unappreciated, or invisible.

- Losing yourself in other people's needs, drama, or demands.

Does this sound familiar? This is not a flaw in your personality. It's a signal: **you've outgrown people-pleasing.** Empowerment means reclaiming your inner authority, and it starts with saying: *"I no longer abandon myself to make others comfortable."*

Boundaries Are Rooted in Integrity

There is a deep connection between boundaries and integrity. Integrity means living in alignment with **your truth** - even when it's uncomfortable. Boundaries are what keep that alignment intact. Every time you honour a boundary, you're saying:

- *"I am worthy of peace."*
- *"I value my needs."*
- *"I trust my inner voice."*

It also means that you live from the inside out, instead of letting the outside dictate who you should be.

Common Boundary Myths (and Truths)

So, let's lovingly dismantle the limiting beliefs that keep us from setting powerful boundaries:

- **Myth:** *"Setting boundaries is selfish."*
  Truth: Honouring your energy helps you show

up more fully and authentically. That's service, not selfishness.

- **Myth:** *"People will be upset with me."*
  Truth: Some will. And that's okay. People who benefit from your lack of boundaries may resist your growth.

- **Myth:** *"I need to explain or justify my boundaries."*
  Truth: Your boundary doesn't need an apology or a paragraph. Clarity is enough.

- **Myth:** *"If I set boundaries, I'll lose love."*
  Truth: Real love respects boundaries. If love disappears because you've chosen self-respect, it wasn't love - it was control.

How to Begin Setting Soul-Aligned Boundaries

You can set soul-aligned boundaries to confirm who you are, and not be dictated to by others, who might want to dictate who you are. Here are some steps to help you establish powerful, clear, and heart-centred boundaries:

1. Get Honest About Your Needs

To begin with, you cannot set boundaries if you don't know what you need. You need to be clear about what you want for yourself, and in doing so, you should reflect on the following three questions, to get a clear sense of where to set your boundaries. You can ask yourself these sample questions:

- *Where in my life do I feel drained, frustrated, or resentful?*
- *What part of me is being neglected or ignored?*
- *What would help me feel safe, seen, and supported?*

As you evaluate the answers, be confident that your needs are not a burden - they are a compass, that will guide you to navigate where the boundaries are set, and what those boundaries are.

2. Communicate with Clarity and Compassion

One of the first thing to realise is that you don't need to be harsh - you just need to be clear as you communicate preferences. Some expressions of being clear could be:

- *"I'm not available for that right now."*
- *"I need time to recharge, so I'm not attending."*
- *"I love you, and I need some space to process."*

You will discover that with clarity, your confidence will come from owning your boundary without shrinking. And most importantly, you don't have to explain your worth to anyone; all that is needed is for you to express your truth to yourself.

3. Expect Discomfort (But Stay Rooted)

Setting boundaries, especially if it's new, can feel uncomfortable at first. You may feel guilt, anxiety, or fear of rejection but that's okay. It's not a sign you're doing it wrong. It's a sign you're breaking patterns of self-abandonment. Go ahead and stand tall. Speak gently. Breathe through the discomfort, and remember, temporary discomfort creates long-term peace.

4. Follow Through Without Wavering

As you make changes, set your boundaries and follow through with clarity, don't be surprised that this new reality may cause others to test your resolve. Remember, a boundary is only as strong as your willingness to uphold it. So, if someone tests or ignores it, you don't need to fight. You must simply **re-affirm**.

- "I understand that's how you feel. This is still my decision."
- "I'm not able to do that, even if it's inconvenient."
- "I've communicated my limit, and I'm standing by it."

The key in setting boundaries is being consistent, because **consistency** is both the action and language of power.

5. Make Peace with the Shifts

When you start honouring your boundaries, your life will shift. Some relationships may fade, some roles may dissolve, but something else will rise in their place - **Your peace. Your self-trust. Your clarity.** You are not losing anything essential; you are clearing space for alignment.

6. Sacred Boundary Reflection & Practice

As you continue your journey to tapping the power within, setting your boundaries and reflecting on your practices, you should take a few moments daily and reflect with these questions:

- *Where in my life have I been saying yes when I really mean no?*
- *What boundary is my soul asking me to set?*
- *What would it look like to protect my peace without guilt?*
- *What support do I need as I step into this?*

As you reflect on these daily, you should write your answers without judgment. Let this be an honest, sacred check-in with yourself.

Boundaries Are Acts of Love

Finally, boundaries are indeed acts of love – that of setting out how you should be treated and how you should also treat yourself. The more you honour your energy, the more magnetic and clear you become. Not only that, but people will also know where you stand. Most important, you know who you are. You stop bending to fit into spaces that no longer hold your spirit – and **that is freedom.** Boundaries are not just about saying *no* to others - they are about saying *yes* to your soul. So, protect your peace and honour your truth. Let your life become a reflection of your deepest integrity.

CHAPTER 11
Navigating Fear – From Paralysis to Power

In Chapter 3, we highlighted the fear of failure as a roadblock to self-empowerment and looked at the solutions for overcoming and dealing with it. What was clear from this earlier discussion, is that some aspects of fear can be regarded as a natural part of growth. It is not altogether a sign of weakness, but a signal: *you're standing at the edge of expansion.* The fact is everyone who chooses the path of empowerment encounters fear. The difference isn't whether fear exists - it's **how we choose to move through it**. Remember fear is not your enemy, it can be seen as your invitation to step into something greater.

The Gift Hidden in Fear

Fear is often misunderstood. It's not just about danger; it's about **perceived risk**. The ego fears change, loss, rejection, the unknown, but your **soul craves evolution.** When you feel fear rising, it's often because you're about to step outside of your comfort zone. It may also be to do with the fact that you're expanding into unfamiliar territory, or that you're releasing a pattern that once kept you *"safe."*

But fear can mean you're growing, and although Chapter 1 provides a greater depth discussion on the manifestations of fear, let's break down three types of fear here, and most importantly, how we can transform them into **power:** along your empowerment journey.

Three Types of Fear on the Empowerment Journey

1. **The Fear of Not Being Enough**
   Rooted in comparison, imposter syndrome, and old wounds. It whispers, *"Who do you think you are?"*

2. **The Fear of Rejection or Abandonment**
   This fear arises when setting boundaries, speaking your truth, or being authentic. It asks, *"Will they still love me?"*

3. **The Fear of Failure**
   The fear of failure can prevent you from taking bold steps, risks, or attempting creative expressions. It warns, *"What if this doesn't work out?"*

Looking at these three fears you will notice that none of them really are the end. They are simply thresholds, and as we explore these below, you will learn how to transform these fears into power.

How to Transform Fear into Power

Here are some steps to help you transition from fear to fully harnessing and accepting your inner power. These steps, grounded in the **Self-Empowerment Excellence Model (SEEM),**© are profound because when you develop the **self-awareness** to get to the root of what's making you fearful, you begin to access the dormant power within you - the part that is capable of transforming fear into fuel. By applying **self-discipline** and cultivating a **positive mindset**, you can face fearful situations not with avoidance, but with strength, clarity, and purpose.

1. Name It Without Judgment

Fear has the most control when it's vague and unspoken. But with **self-awareness**, you can bring it into the light. Ask yourself: *What exactly am I afraid of?* and *What is this fear trying to protect me from?* Naming your fear clearly and without self-judgment loosens its grip, and gives you the power to respond consciously, rather than reactively.

2. Thank It, Then Lead Anyway

Often, fear shows up as a protective mechanism. Honouring that part of you requires both **compassion** and **discipline**. With loving acknowledgment, say:

"Thank you for trying to protect me. But I choose growth now."

This is where **self-discipline** empowers you to move forward - not by eliminating fear, but by choosing to lead yourself through it anyway.

3. Take One Aligned Step

You don't need to have it all figured out - just the next step. Confidence doesn't arise from fearlessness, but from taking aligned action in the presence of fear. With a **positive mindset**, you begin to trust that even small, courageous steps will create momentum. Each act of bravery strengthens your belief in yourself, reinforcing your empowered identity. Then by engaging these steps with **awareness**, **discipline**, and a **mindset** of possibility, fear becomes less of a barrier and more of a guide - pointing you directly toward your next breakthrough.

4. Breathe Into the Body – *Let's Practice Now!*

As mentioned earlier, fear lives in the body; this can be felt as trapped energy. So, to combat it you should release it by moving, stretching or grounding yourself. At the same time, let your breath become your anchor in uncertain waters.

Below, I will take you through one way you can use your breath to move from fear and resistance to effortless momentum. Know that transformation begins with aligning yourself with the universal energies, and alignment begins with what you say frequently.

For example, here is an affirmation statement that will lead us into a breath exercise to eliminate fear. It will be said during the breath meditation, when you say it, do so with conviction:

"I step into the current of grace, I'm not afraid; all the courage I need now flows through me."

Announcing your alignment is taking ownership of your affirmation. For example, saying the words, *"I step into..."* is an act of sovereign choice and then the phrase *"current of grace,"* acknowledges that you trust the universe's intelligence which operates beyond your schedule. *"Grace"* is never too early and never too late. It is precise and by stepping into it, you move from resistance to effortless momentum. Furthermore, the phrase, *"all the courage I need"* is a statement of trust. It confirms that you trust there is a higher plan; a destiny you're meant to fulfil. The words, *"now flows to me."* is about radical receptivity. You don't need to hunt for it – it is being done as it is expressed.

You only need to **become an open channel**. And the idea of receiving, is about trust. It's a silent certainty that you are no longer arguing with your own destiny. When you speak this command, you must do it with absolute presence. Allow each word to resonate, speak into the very air around you, as if it's already a fact. You must repeat it as many times as necessary, until it feels true in your body. It should not be forced, not mechanical; just known. **The universe is always aware, it's always listening** for those who know how to speak with clarity, peace and authority. Therefore, when it hears that command spoken, from your spirit, it will respond.

Before you speak the words from the affirmation statement above, find a moment of stillness. Let the world outside fade away - no music, no interruptions; just you, your breath and the powerful frequency that's already gathering around you. As you prepare to express yourself, know that the silence is not empty; it's full, it's the sacred space where true transformation takes place.

Silence sends its own signal. By choosing silence, you attune your energy field in a way that noise can never permit. You start to feel your reality, instead of just thinking about it. That is the first step that moves you **from head to your heart.** Worries or doubts may try to surface, but don't entertain them. Observe them and just let them drift by without engaging them. You don't need to do battle in your mind, just stop giving worry your precious energy. The quieter your mind, the clearer your signal to the universal energies will be, and the surer your manifestation will be from the expressed command.

The Breath work in practice

Here is a word of advice. Before you start, be sure that you are in a safe place - not driving or operating any machinery!

Let's begin:

Wherever you are, gently close your eyes... or soften your gaze. Begin by noticing your breath, the gentle rise and fall of your chest as you breathe in cool air and breathe out warm air - don't change it yet; just notice it.

Now slowly breathe in... through your nose.

Hold it for a moment... and then exhale through your mouth.

Let's do that again.

Inhale...

Hold...

Exhale .... slowly.

Let your shoulders drop. Relax your hands and soften your jaw. You're safe here.

Now, place a hand over your heart. This is your anchor of truth – this is where your words will find their real power. Not from the sound of your voice but from the coherence between your heart and mind. As your hand rests on your chest, your awareness will turn inward, and you will begin to feel your own energetic presence. And this is all that's required – not perfection but presence.

Now, inhale deeply and hold that breath for a count of three. Feel the stillness in that pause, then exhale completely.

That single breath informs your nervous system that you are safe; and when your body is safe, your energy becomes receptive. That's the moment your spoken command will have an impact, because it's not rushed but anchored.

Feel your heart beating. That's your life-force. Feel your chest rise and fall. Your heart's beating...quietly...faithfully. Now move your awareness to your arms.... Then to your hands... Notice where you are holding anything – emotionally or physically - let it go.

Now feel the weight of your body, where it's supported underneath you. Your legs... your feet... connecting with the earth beneath you. You're grounded. You are supported. You are safe in this moment. Take a breath in and gently let it go.

This is not a show, it's a connection. There is no need for special candles, perfect music or ceremonies. All that's required is your authenticity. That is the point where the universe meets you in your truth. Feel the potency of the moment as you speak. Allow the intention to build organically. Now you are ready to state or affirm your intention:

"I step into the current of grace, I'm not afraid; all the courage I need now flows through me."

Let the words rise, not from your ego, but from that quiet knowing place.

Now, take a deep breath in, and slowly release through your mouth.

Inhale... And exhale... gently. Repeat this quiet breathing 3 x times.

This peace, this stillness you created, lives in you. Know that it's always available to you, and you can return here anytime you need to. Inhale.... Exhale... repeat these 3 x times.

As we bring this breath session to a close, you are now going to bring awareness back to this moment. Wiggle your fingers...Roll your shoulders. Take one last deep, nourishing breath.

Inhale... Exhale.... Then as you come back to awareness in your body, say this affirmation:

"I'm at peace. I trust in the universe and wait for its blessings. Thank you, Universe."

Saying *"thanks" is* a way of showing gratitude. When you start to live with a grateful heart, something beautiful happens. You begin to see more, feel more, and appreciate more. Gratitude changes your energy, and that energy touches the people around you. It's a practice, not a one-time event. And like any meaningful habit, the more you nurture it, the more it nurtures you.

In summary, you have just transitioned from fear to power, you acknowledged with authenticity where you were. But as you affirmed your statement, took charge of the narrative, with courageous steps, it confirmed that you did not make fear your master; instead, you mastered it.

Continue to stay in your truth and power!

PART IV –
EXPANSION AND CONTRIBUTION

CHAPTER 12
Creating a Vision – Aligning with Your Future Self

This chapter is not about fantasy. It's about energetic alignment. Empowerment requires direction, and direction needs clarity. When you craft a clear vision for your life, you align with your **future self.** Your future self is the version of you that's already living in wholeness, abundance, peace, and purpose. You're not just healing - you're **becoming**.

Why Vision Matters

Having a vision for your life matters, because without vision, life pulls you in many directions. You become reactive, not intentional. With vision, you make decisions with clarity, you also attract aligned opportunities, and you rise into the vibration of who you are becoming. Overall, vision gives your energy a focus point with which you can connect to envision your future. As you learn to connect with yourself, you will notice that your future self is not a stranger. Your future self already exists energetically, because it is an embodiment of what's possible. So, take a moment to imagine what your empowered life will look like, by asking these questions:

- *How do you feel when you wake up?*
- *What kind of boundaries do you uphold?*
- *How do you speak, lead, create, and love?*

This isn't about achieving perfection, it's about creating a vision and **embodying alignment** in your life. I set out below some creative ways of crafting a living vision as follows:

1. **Write It Out** – Describe your future in the present tense.
   "I am grounded. I trust myself. I live with joy and clarity."

2. **Anchor It Emotionally** – Feel the emotions now. Gratitude, peace, excitement.
   The vibration is more important than the details.

3. **Visualize Regularly** – See it. Feel it. Speak it aloud.
   Let your subconscious align with what you repeatedly focus on.

From Vision to Embodiment

As you connect to your future self, you should know that it is not enough to just imagine what it would be like. You must also ask yourself questions, to gain clarity of purpose, which would be based on the answers that you get. Sample questions can be as follows:

- *What choices will my future-self make today?*
- *How can I show up now as the person I'm becoming?*

And remember, you don't become your vision by waiting; you become your vision by living in alignment with it now - moment by moment. This begins with **self-awareness** - deeply understanding who you are, what you value, and what truly matters to you. When you're aware of your internal landscape, you can navigate life with more clarity and intention.

If you want to take it to the next level, why not write a short, soulful **Vision Statement** of who you are becoming? This Vision Statement can then become your guide for your subsequent actions. You can begin with the following starter:

"I am a calm, clear, and confident woman/man/person. I trust my path. I create with purpose. I lead with love."

But vision alone is not enough. Relating this need back to our **Self-Empowerment Excellence Model (SEEM)**,© you will realise that it takes **self-discipline** to show up each day in alignment with that vision - to make choices that reflect your future self, even when it's challenging. And it takes a ***positive***

mindset to believe in your growth, to reframe setbacks as lessons, and to stay inspired through the process.

Ultimately, moving from vision to embodiment means more than just imagining a better version of yourself - it requires becoming that version through intentional action. By aligning your daily habits, choices, and mindset with the future you aspire to be, you bridge the gap between who you are now, and who you're becoming.

Vision is the starting point, but embodiment is the lived truth; it's where *clarity meets commitment*. When you consistently show up as your future self, rooted in **self-awareness,** guided by **self-discipline**, and fuelled by a **positive mindset**; then transformation becomes not just possible - but inevitable.

CHAPTER 13
Empowered Relationships – Leading with Love & Truth

This chapter is not about changing others. It's about **changing how you relate** - from fear and performance to love and truth. True self-empowerment doesn't isolate; it elevates. It reshapes how we show up in relationships, not by controlling others, but by choosing radical authenticity. When you become empowered, your relationships evolve: some deepen, some dissolve and some transform in ways you never imagined.

Empowered Relationships Begin with You

The most important relationship you'll ever have is with yourself. This is when you speak kindly to yourself, honour your boundaries and listen to your inner truth. In fact, you naturally attract people who meet you, at that vibration. Having already discussed this under self-compassion, you will remember that we focused on teaching others how to treat us, by the way we also treat ourselves.

The signs of Empowered Relationships embody having an open and honest communication - without manipulation or fear. Other signs include mutual respect for space, growth, and autonomy, love that liberates rather than confines, and boundaries that strengthen connection - not sever it.

As you navigate your self-empowerment journey, know that empowered relationships are not perfect - they are *conscious*. They are also rooted in truth, not performance. They are also rooted in presence, not pretending.

Transforming Old Patterns

Most of us were conditioned to seek approval, avoid conflict, or shrink ourselves to be liked. However, empowered love doesn't demand performance, it invites presence. You must release the following habits – people-pleasing, emotional caretaking and fear of rejection. Instead, you should choose truth-telling, sacred listening and sovereign connection. Below are three practices for conscious relationships:

1. **Speak Your Truth with Compassion**
   Say what's real for you without blame or defence. This is because truth heals and avoidance festers.

2. **Hold Space Without Fixing**
   Let people have their emotions. You don't need to solve them, just witness with love.

3. **Celebrate Without Comparison**
   Remember that empowerment thrives when we uplift each other; without competition.

Here are some reflection questions to ask yourself as you transition from old patterns to a more empowered way of living.

1. *Where in my life am I withholding my truth in relationships?*
2. *What patterns of people-pleasing or emotional caretaking am I ready to release?*
3. *What would it feel like to show up fully as myself - with no performance?*
4. *Who in my life models empowered, conscious connection?*
5. *How can I create space for deeper authenticity in my relationships starting today?*

Finally, in applying our **Self-Empowerment Excellence Model (SEEM)**©, to these empowered relationships, confirms that transforming old patterns in relationships begins with radical **self-awareness** and a willingness to meet ourselves with compassion. It means that with **self-discipline**, you are no longer reacting from wounds, projections, or inherited narratives, but choosing to respond from a place of clarity, sovereignty, and emotional maturity.

In empowered relationships, people with a **positive mindset,** take responsibility for their inner landscapes, allowing intimacy to grow, not through control or co-dependency, but through honesty, respect, and mutual growth.

As we shed outdated behaviours and step into conscious relating, we create space for love that is not bound by fear but anchored in truth. This transformation is not about perfection - it's about presence, accountability, and the shared courage to evolve, together.

CHAPTER 14
The Ripple Effect – Living as a Lighthouse

When we choose to live in alignment with our truth, grounded in presence and purpose, we naturally become a beacon for others - not by force, but by embodiment. Like a lighthouse, we don't chase ships; we simply shine. This quiet radiance creates a ripple effect, touching lives in ways we may never fully see. Living as a lighthouse means committing to our own inner clarity so that others can find their way more easily. It's a powerful reminder that our personal growth is never just personal - it becomes a light that helps to guide others home.

Similarly, Empowerment is not just about your personal growth. It's about your **energetic impact**. You are a lighthouse. You don't chase boats - you stand firmly, shining your light. When you live from wholeness, you inspire others to do the same. You break cycles for generations and you become a safe space in a chaotic world.

Why Your Growth Matters to the Collective

Every act of self-healing radiates outward, and when you set a boundary, others learn it's okay to have needs. When you speak your truth, you give permission to others and when you choose peace over performance, you shift the frequency of your environment. The fact is, you are not just healing yourself; you're **elevating your consciousness.**

You Are an Answered Prayer

Although you may not be aware of it, as you go about your daily life, someone is watching you, and your transformation helps them to appreciate and remember what's possible. In fact, your courage plants a seed of transformation in people you may never meet. And your presence, more than your perfection, is the gift. In other words, you become the energy you cultivate. You do this by being the calm you seek; being the truth you crave, and the love you were waiting for. When you embody what you once needed, you no longer chase healing; you **become the medicine.**

Finally, to live as a lighthouse is to trust that your steady light matters - even when no one says so, even when the waves are rough. It begins with **self-awareness**: knowing your values, your presence, and the quiet strength you offer. When you stand in your truth, aware of your energy and impact, you become a silent yet powerful force of inspiration.

It also takes **self-discipline** to remain aligned with your integrity, especially in moments of doubt or fatigue. Choosing to shine consistently, without needing recognition, is a courageous act of devotion to your purpose. It's not about perfection, but about returning - again and again - to your values and vision, even when it's inconvenient.

And throughout it all, a **positive mindset** becomes the anchor that keeps you grounded. Rather than seeking applause, you trust that your authenticity plants seeds, that your ripple will reach shores unseen. You embody hope, grace, and quiet leadership - not by demanding change, but by *being* it.

The ripple effect of living authentically is subtle yet profound, inspiring others not through instruction, but through embodied example. As you continue to lead with presence and alignment, consider the following reflection questions, to deepen your self-empowerment journey:

1. What energetic impact do I want to have on others?
2. How has my own growth already influenced those around me?
3. What fears (if any) do I hold around being seen, leading, or standing out?

4. How can I embody more of what I wish the world had more of - starting with me?
5. Where am I being called to shine my light, without needing validation or applause?

In a world often lost in noise and distraction, your being grounded becomes an invitation: to slow down, to wake up, to come home. And that in itself, is an act of quiet revolution, as is highlighted by our **Self-Empowerment Excellence Model (SEEM)**©. It is because that quiet revolution is rooted in **self-awareness,** sustained by **self-discipline,** and lit by a resilient, **positive mindset.**

CHAPTER 15
Full Circle – Becoming the Embodied Self

There comes a moment on the path where seeking gives way to integration - when the insights we've gathered, the healing we've done, and the truths we've touched are no longer ideas we chase, but ways of being we live. This is the journey of coming full circle: not returning to where we started, but arriving with new depth, wisdom, and embodiment.

Becoming the embodied self means honouring the sacred within the everyday, allowing your lived experience to reflect your inner truth. It's not about perfection or arrival - it's about wholeness, rooted presence, and a deep remembering of who you've always been beneath the layers. This is where the real journey begins - not upward or outward, but inward, home to yourself.

So, a self-discovery fact must be that this journey is not about fixing yourself. It's about **returning to your wholeness.** You were never broken - only disconnected. You were never lost - only asleep to your power. Now, you remember. You have returned to your voice, your clarity, your boundaries, your vision. You are no longer living in reaction - you are **choosing with intention.** And that is intention of integration and intention over information. Therefore, Empowerment isn't about knowing more, it's about **living differently.**

So, let this not be just another book you read, but a life you embody. You should, practice the presence, live the boundaries, speak the truth, trust the vision and lead with love. An important factor to consider also is based on a landmark study undertaken by the University College London (Lally et al, 2010), which states that the average time to form a new habit is 6 days, with the full range of habit formation taking anywhere from 18 to 254 days. This highlights the importance of consistency, patience and time in rewiring the brain, as it adapts to its new messaging from your empowered actions.

As we come to the closing moments of this book, you can now reflect on the following questions, as you personally evaluate how you were brought here.

1. What has shifted within me since I began this journey?
2. Which tools, practices, or lessons do I want to carry forward into daily life?
3. In what areas of my life am I ready to embody more alignment and self-trust?

4. What does living as my most empowered, embodied self-look and feel like?
5. What daily rituals or reminders can help me stay connected to this version of myself?

To come full circle is not to finish the journey, but to begin truly *living* it - fully, consciously, and from within. The embodied self no longer seeks to escape or transcend life but meets it with grounded presence and unwavering truth.

In this space, you will agree that the **Self-Empowerment Excellence Model (SEEM)**©, applied to your journey of transformation, is truly shaped by **self-awareness**. We no longer perform who we think we *should* be; we simply inhabit who we *are*. Every experience, every lesson, every moment has been an invitation into deeper knowing and becoming.

Rooted in this awareness and aligned with our essence, we now walk forward - not as seekers, but as living, breathing expressions of the wholeness we've reclaimed. This is where **self-discipline** takes root: the daily commitment to return to your truth, to choose alignment over distraction, and to act with integrity even when it's hard.

The circle completes - not as an end, but as a return to self, to source, to home.

This is just the beginning of your self-empowerment journey. It affirms that your inner power isn't a destination - it's a way of being. And it's sustained by a **positive mindset**: one that believes in growth, embraces imperfection, and sees each day as a fresh opportunity to return, refine, and re-align. This is because ultimately, your power does not come from what you do - it comes from who you choose to *be*, moment by moment.

And when you forget? Come home again. The tools are within you - always.

Here's my parting blessing to you:

"May you walk in clarity, courage and awareness.
May your voice be clear and your mind remain strong.
May your presence be a sanctuary - for yourself and for others.
*And may you always remember that **you** are the light you've been searching for."*

Roselle Thompson

CHAPTER 16
30-DAY EMPOWERMENT CHALLENGE

Daily Practices for Clarity, Courage & Self-Alignment

"Empowerment isn't a one-time decision - it's a way of living. Every day is an opportunity to return to your power."

Committing to this 30-Day Empowerment Challenge is more than just a personal goal - it's an intentional act of self-leadership. In a world that often pulls our attention outward, this challenge invites you to turn inward and consciously reclaim your power, clarity, and direction. Through small, consistent daily actions, you'll begin to shift patterns, build confidence, and strengthen the connection to your authentic self. It's not about achieving perfection - it's about showing up, again and again, with presence and purpose.

These 30 days are a gateway: a chance to reset, realign, and remember the strength that's already within you.

How to Use This Challenge:

- Set aside **10–20 minutes daily**.
- Keep a **journal** to track your reflections.

- Move at your own pace - but aim for **consistency over perfection**.
- Return to any challenge that resonates deeply.

WEEK 1: RETURNING TO YOUR TRUTH

Day 1: Define Empowerment
What does being *"empowered"* mean to *you*? Write your own definition. Speak it aloud.

Day 2: Voice Activation
Say something today that you've been holding back (with love and honesty).

Day 3: Power Inventory
List 5 ways you've given your power away recently. Reclaim each with intention.

Day 4: Inner Child Check-In
Write a letter to your younger self. What do they need to hear from you?

Day 5: Clear One Boundary
Identify one boundary you've been avoiding and honour it today.

Day 6: Fear Journaling
What fear is currently holding you back? Name it. Witness it. Breathe into it.

Day 7: Silence + Stillness
Spend 10–15 minutes in complete stillness. No distractions. Just presence.

WEEK 2: EMBODYING SELF-LOVE

Day 8: Mirror Work
Look into your eyes in the mirror. Say: *"I trust you. I honour you. I love you."*

Day 9: Self-Celebration
Celebrate 3 things you're proud of - big or small. Own your growth.

Day 10: Body Blessing
Instead of criticising your body, thank it today. Touch it with love.

Day 11: Let Something Go
Release one thing - an object, a habit, or thought - that no longer serves.

Day 12: Say No with Grace
Say "no" where you usually say "yes" out of guilt or fear.

Day 13: Sacred Space Reset
Declutter or beautify a small space to feel energetically aligned.

Day 14: Digital Detox Hour
Unplug for 1 hour. Do something nurturing, creative, or still.

WEEK 3: EMPOWERED VISION + ACTION

Day 15: Future Self Visualization
Journal: *Who is the empowered version of me? How do they speak, act, and live?*

Day 16: Aligned Action Step
Take one bold step toward a goal or vision - even if it's small.

Day 17: Speak Your Vision
Share your dream/vision with someone safe or say it out loud in private.

Day 18: Clear all the *"Shoulds"*
Notice and release 3 *"shoulds"* driving your choices today.

Day 19: Rewrite a Limiting Belief
Choose one limiting belief and reframe it.

Day 20: Embodied Movement
Dance, stretch, walk - move your body intuitively for 10–20 minutes.

Day 21: Gratitude as Power
Write a list of 10 things you're grateful for - and *feel* each one.

WEEK 4: LIVING ALIGNED & UNAPOLOGETIC

Day 22: The Authentic YES
Say "yes" only where your soul aligns. Notice how it feels in your body.

Day 23: Radical Rest
Give yourself permission to rest without guilt. What nourishes your nervous system?

Day 24: Intuition Check-In
Ask: *What is my inner wisdom guiding me toward today?* Follow it.

Day 25: Release Comparison
Unfollow, mute, or let go of anything that triggers comparison today.

Day 26: Honour Your Energy Cycles
Reflect: *When do I feel most alive, creative, peaceful?* Adjust your schedule to honour it.

Day 27: Self-Trust Anchor
Recall 3 moments where trusting yourself paid off. Write a mantra: *"I can trust myself."*

Day 28: Soul Nourishment
Do one thing today *just* because it brings you joy. No productivity required.

Day 29: Empowerment Letter
Write a letter from your empowered self to your present self. Let it guide and inspire.

Day 30: Claim Your Becoming
Declare: *"I am not who I was. I am becoming who I truly am."* Write your new personal power statement.

Final Reflection

Take a moment to reflect on the last 30 days by asking yourself these questions:

- *What shifted?*
- *What expanded?*
- *What awakened?*
- *Who have you become?*

You are your own best guide. Return to these practices as often as needed. Your empowerment is always just one choice away.

REFERENCES

1. **Dr. Candace Pert,** an American Neuroscientist and Pharmacologist who discovered the opioid receptor, the cellular binding site for endorphins in the brain. *Neuropeptides and their Receptors: A Psychosomatic Network*, J. Immunology Vol.135:820s-826s, (1985).

2. **Dr. Norman Doidge,** A Canadian psychiatrist, psychoanalyst and Author of *The Brain that Changs Itself* (2007) & *The Brain's Way of Healing*, (2015).

3. **Dr. James Pennebaker,** an American social psychologist, Professor Emeritus of Psychology at the University of Texas at Austin. *The Healing Power of Expressing Emotions*, (1997).

4. **Dr. Roberts Emmons,** an American psychologist and Professor at UC Davis, California, is Author of *The Little Book of Gratitude* (2016), *Gratitude Works!* (2013) & *Thanks! How the New Science of Gratitude Can Make You Happier* (2007).

5. **Dr. Carol Dweck,** A Stanford Psychologist & Professor of Psychology: Growth Mindset Pioneer and Author of *Mindset: How you can Fulfil your Potential* (2012) & *Mindset: The New Psychology of Success*, (2006).

6. **Dr. Kristin Neff,** Associate Professor in Psychology at the University of Texas. Author of *Self-Compassion: The Proven Power of Being Kind to Yourself* (co-ed) *The Mindful Self-Compassion Workbook* (2018) & *Teaching the Mindful Self-Compassion Program: A guide for Professionals,* (2019).

7. **Dr. Phillippa Lally et al;** *How are habits formed: Modelling habit formation in the real world.* University College London, (2010).

8. **Dr. Joe Dispenza,** *Breaking the Habit of Being Yourself,* (2012).

9. **Dr. Fred Luskin,** Stanford University's Forgiveness Project; *Forgive for Good* (2003) & *Forgive for Love,* (2009)

10. **Dr. Shad Helmstetter,** Stanford psychologists and cognitive neuroscientists. *What to Say When You Talk to Yourself,* (1991)

RECOMMENDED READING & RESOURCES

"Healing and empowerment are ongoing journeys. Let the wisdom of others walk beside you."

Personal Growth & Empowerment

1. **The Gifts of Imperfection** by Brené Brown
2. **Atomic Habits** by James Clear
3. **You Are a Badass** by Jen Sincero
4. **The Mountain Is You** by Brianna Wiest
5. **Radical Acceptance** by Tara Brach

Mindset & Psychology

1. **Mindset: The New Psychology of Success** by Carol S. Dweck
2. **The Four Agreements** by Don Miguel Ruiz
3. **The Untethered Soul** by Michael A. Singer
4. **The Power of Now** by Eckhart Tolle
5. **Emotional Agility** by Susan David

Spiritual & Energetic Alignment

1. **A Return to Love** by Marianne Williamson
2. **Light Is the New Black** by Rebecca Campbell
3. **Sacred Woman** by Queen Afua
4. **The Seat of the Soul** by Gary Zukav
5. **Journey of Souls** by Michael Newton

Self-Compassion & Healing

1. **Self-Compassion** by Kristin Neff
2. **Attached** by Amir Levine & Rachel Heller

3. **Women Who Run with the Wolves** by Clarissa Pinkola Estés
4. **The Body Keeps the Score** by Bessel van der Kolk
5. **It Didn't Start with You** by Mark Wolynn

Journaling & Practice Tools

1. **The Artist's Way** by Julia Cameron
2. **The Five-Minute Journal** by Intelligent Change
3. **The Desire Map** by Danielle LaPorte
4. **Letting Go: The Pathway of Surrender** by David R. Hawkins

Podcasts & Audio Resources

1. *Roselle Empowerment School TV* by Roselle Thompson
2. *On Being* with Krista Tippett
3. *Unlocking Us* by Brené Brown
4. *The Mind Valley Podcast*
5. *Therapy Chat* with Laura Reagan
6. *The Lively Show* with Jess Lively
7. *The Rose Sanctuary* -YouTube Channel - (@the_rose_sanctuary

Additional Tools & Resources

1. **Insight Timer** (Meditation & Sleep App)
2. **Headspace** (Mindfulness App)
3. **To Be Magnetic** (Inner Work & Manifestation Tools)
4. **The Pattern/Co-star** (Self-awareness Astrology Apps)
5. **Journaling apps** like Day One or Journey
6. **The Rose Sanctuary:**
   Facebook
   https://facebook.com/therosesanctuary1
   Instagram
   www.instagram.com/the_rose_sanctuary
   YouTube
   www.youtube.com/@theRoseSanctuary1

Your Personal Toolkit
Remember: no resource is more powerful than your own inner wisdom. Use these tools not to replace your intuition, but to amplify your access to it.

BOOKS BY THE SAME AUTHOR:

- *Papa Bois: King of Paradise (2022)*
- *Poems to Navigate Caribbean Diaspora Disruptions (2021)*
- *The Phantom of the Great House (2021)*
- *Gang-Gang Sarah: A Caribbean Sensation (2020)*
- *Shakespeare for Children: Macbeth (2020)*
- *11+ English Preparation Tests for the CEM Exam 2020*
- *Phonics & Spelling Workbook 1 (2020)*
- *Rhythms of Life: An Anthology of Modern Poetry (2019)*
- *Mastering Comprehension Skills (2019)*
- *The New Caribbean Folktales and Legends for the 21st Century (2018)*
- *English Grammar: A Student's Companion (2018)*
- *Vocabulary Skills for Students & Teachers: A Practical Learning Toolkit (2018)*
- *Spelling &* Word-Power Skills Volume 1 (2018)*
- *A Woman of Destiny: A Calypso Novel (2015)*
- *A Woman of Destiny: The Text Study Guide (2015)*
- *T A Marryshow CBE – Honouring Caribbean Greats (2001)*

EAGLE PUBLICATIONS

www.ingramcontent.com/pod-product-compliance
Lightning Source LLC
Chambersburg PA
CBHW052016070526
44584CB00016B/1776